Ezra Pound and the Erotic Medium

Ezra Pound and the Erotic Medium

Kevin Oderman

Duke University Press   1986   *Durham*

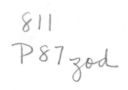

Previously unpublished material by Ezra Pound is copyright
© 1986 by the Trustees of the Ezra Pound Literary Property Trust
and Faber & Faber, Ltd. Reprinted by permission of New
Directions Publishing Corporation, New York, and by Faber & Faber,
London.

Part of "A Maple Tree in Pennsylvania" previously appeared as " 'The Sort
of Remembering that is Reality,' " in *Denver Quarterly*, vol. 14, no. 3, pp.
117–19. Reprinted by permission.

"Servants of Amor: The Early Poetry" previously appeared in a slightly
different version as "The Servants of Amor in Pound's Early Poems," in
Paideuma, vol. 8, no. 3, pp. 389–403. Reprinted by permission.

Part of "Divagation: Physiology" previously appeared in a slightly different
version as "Of Vision, Tennis Courts, and Glands," in *Paideuma*, vol. 13,
no. 2, pp. 253–60. Reprinted by permission.

" 'Cavalcanti': That the Body is not Evil" and part of "The Cantos: Second
Assay" previously appeared in slightly different versions as " 'Cavalcanti':
That the Body is not Evil" in *Paideuma*, vol. 11, no. 2, pp. 257–79. Re-
printed by permission.

"A Girl," "Sub Mare," and "The Tree," in Ezra Pound, *Collected Early
Poems*. Copyright © 1976 by The Trustees of the Ezra Pound Literary
Property Trust and Faber & Faber, Ltd. All rights reserved. Reprinted by
permission.

"Heather" and "Shop Girl," in Ezra Pound, *Personae*. Copyright 1926 by
Ezra Pound. Reprinted by permission of New Directions Publishing Corporation, New York, and by Faber & Faber, Ltd., London.

Permission to quote from Ezra Pound manuscript material held in the Collection of American Literature, Beinecke Rare Book and Manuscript Library,
Yale University, is gratefully acknowledged.

for CO, who suffered the
absences and the presences
senesco sed amo

Contents

Abbreviations

I have cited the books of Ezra Pound in the conventional manner, to identify the edition I have used, for the first citation only. Thereafter, citations appear in the text. I have adopted the abbreviations standardized by Carroll F. Terrell, in *Paideuma* and *A Companion to the Cantos of Ezra Pound*. *The Cantos* are cited by canto number and page only, hence (17/76) refers to Canto 17, page 76.

CEP   *Collected Early Poems*
GB   *Gaudier-Brzeska: A Memoir*
GK   *Guide to Kulchur*
L   *Letters of Ezra Pound*
LE   *Literary Essays*
NPL   Postscript to *Natural Philosophy of Love*
P   *Personae: Collected Shorter Poems*
SP   *Selected Prose*
SR   *Spirit of Romance*
T   *Translations*

Preface

That there is a visionary dimension in Ezra Pound's frequent but
cryptic references to sexuality in his poetry and prose has long been
apparent to commentators, but just what it is has not received
much scrutiny. In this study, I will demonstrate that Pound, from
very early on, was preoccupied with the "mediumistic" potentialities of sexuality, its ability to stimulate visions. The demonstration hinges on an explication of four central prose texts: "Psychology and Troubadours," the "Translator's Postscript" to Remy
de Gourmont's *The Natural Philosophy of Love*, "The New Therapy," and "Cavalcanti." The results of these explications are
brought to bear first on the early poems and then, in three chapters, on *The Cantos*. Mediumistic sexuality, this investigation suggests, is a major topic of Pound's poetry, though his treatment of
it is "occult"—meant for an elect audience.

The visionary eroticism traced here does not exhaust Pound's
interest in either the erotic or the visionary, and though I argue
for the primacy of "mediumistic sexuality" in any reading of the
"paradisical" passages of *The Cantos*, it remains only one strand in
a web. Nor, it must be said, have I tried to address every passage in
Pound's poetry and prose that bears on my subject. They are too
many. It is my more modest hope that this study will allow readers
to recognize the erotic medium in Pound's work wherever they
meet it. This, in turn, should enable them to make sense of many
passages in *The Cantos* that have previously resisted analysis.

Pound insists, in his treatment of the "visionary colors" of the
erotic, on the sensibility of the lover in "this rite"; he insists as
well, whether he is discussing the Florentine Guido Cavalcanti or
the function of glands, on the element of experience (and on the

experience of experiment).This led me to focus on the experiential dimension of Pound's work, and finally to conclude that Pound, in all his investigations, was prompted by his own experience. This, in turn, prepared me to see a pattern in texts as seemingly disparate as the "Translator's Postscript" and Canto 17. The pattern is there, a singular preoccupation with "mediumistic" sexuality.

I found, in both Pound criticism and my own readings of Pound, that the rationalist presumptions of our criticism, the implicit desire to reduce anything which does not conform to our notions of what constitutes "reality" to something that does, present the critic with a considerable obstacle. I have endeavored to overcome it, to read Pound without a rationalist filter, and I have discovered that he repays the effort. A side of Pound that has been too often blurred in the criticism comes suddenly into focus.

The status of the experiences I'll be discussing is difficult to determine with any finality. While they are certainly visionary, in the sense of seeing things, I would hesitate to describe them as mystical, at least without qualification. The "passion" of the mystic way is in its openness to divine influx. But Pound's passion is not "to suffer," it is to act, to call up visions by performing an erotic rite. I think that such experiences are best described as occult or magical. However, any such distinction is open to question, and I have thus preferred to adopt (and sometimes adapt) Pound's own vocabulary. Still, there is a danger that the conventional definitions of the terminology Pound employs may be interpolated into the reader's understanding of what follows. I have attempted to obviate this possibility by first elucidating the passages in which Pound uses the terms before appropriating them myself, and, second, by the liberal use of quotation marks by way of reminder ("unofficial mysticism"). Finally, this study, in toto, has as object the experience to which the vocabulary of the "erotic medium" refers; in regard to Pound's terminology, then, this book is an extended definition. Bearing all this in mind should keep the language of this study from becoming unnecessarily reductive for the reader.

Acknowledgments

My debt to Ezra Pound scholarship is general and fundamental. Without it, I would not have been able to begin. I have tried in this study to read Pound directly whenever possible, to let Pound comment on Pound, but it is the preparation in Pound scholarship that allowed me to hear him. If there is credit, it must be shared; the errors are mine.

I am particularly indebted to the work of Hugh Kenner. It is not an exaggeration to say that reading *The Pound Era* taught me how to Pound. I would also like to single out the work of Herbert Schneidau, and to thank him for his guidance. Donald Pearce, John Espey, and J. P. Sullivan read all or part of the manuscript and called me back when I strayed.

Sherman Paul's example has reformed, for me, the very idea of scholarship. To thank him is not enough.

Finally, I am grateful to everyone who worked on this book at Duke University Press. They have been both exacting and gracious; I think of them as friends.

Ezra Pound and the Erotic Medium

A Maple Tree in Pennsylvania

Dryad, thy peace is like water Pound, Canto 83

Beginnings are always postulate, and arbitrary. But while I was writing this study what I had taken as the chronological beginning of any analysis of Ezra Pound's visionary eroticism, the publication of *A Lume Spento* in June of 1908, was proven all too arbitrary by the belated appearance of H.D.'s *End to Torment, A Memoir of Ezra Pound*,[1] with its lively account of their romance in Pennsylvania, before Pound embarked for Europe and the Venice which fostered *A Lume Spento*. This "before" was too compelling; it forced me to postulate a new "beginning," in a maple tree in Pennsylvania:

We [Ezra and H.D.] had climbed up into the big maple tree in our garden, outside Philadelphia.

    There was a crow's nest that my younger brother had built— bench boards and a sort of platform. . . . [I prepare] to slide out of the crow's nest.

    "No, Dryad," he says. He snatches me back. We sway with the wind. There is no wind. We sway with the stars. They are not far.[2]

They sway, but the skeptical reader may well see no more in this than the romancing of teenagers, not a subject of critical interest even if the romancers are Ezra Pound and H.D. Indeed, if we had no more than this, skepticism would be well taken. But this is only the first memory to surface, others follow, and in the welling up of memories H.D. largely succeeds, unwittingly or not, in breaking down the partition between the personal and the literary life, both for her and for Pound.[3]

The writing of *End to Torment* was clearly a therapeutic exercise for H.D., a "remembering" of her early and romantic relationship with Ezra in Pennsylvania, which she had subsequently repressed. The stages of this remembering, interleaved with memories from their London years and the contemporary events of 1958, provide a good deal of psychological suspense; but it's the quality of the remembering which really arrests. At one point she writes "this is the sort of remembering that is reality, *ecstasy*,"[4] at another, "It is hardly a process of remembering, but almost, as I have said, of 'manifesting.' "[5] It's almost a birth, although that is not said. However, the reader must suspect an unusual generative process for the book, almost a parentage: "Erich Heydt, the young German *Oberarzt* . . . jabbed an injection needle into my arm. It was perhaps the second or third time that I had seen him—or was it the first? He said, 'You know Ezra Pound, don't you?' This was a shock coming from a stranger. Perhaps he injected me or re-injected me with Ezra."[6] H.D. seems to insist on the Freudian overtones. They would be obvious even if she hadn't recently written her *Tribute to Freud*. If the Freudian cast of this passage is peculiar in the book, the barely submerged sexuality is not. It's a book about sexuality, a particular kind of sexuality.

If the first memories she uncovers are indefinite, just "swaying" in a big maple tree, the later ones are increasingly explicit. They were unlucky, always getting caught, and we are to understand this as the source of her repression. "I was hiding myself and Ezra, standing before my father, caught 'in the very act' you might say. For no 'act' afterwards, though biologically fulfilled, had had the significance of the first *demi-vierge* embraces. The significance of 'first love' can not be overestimated."[7] The "act" here is something passionate, unconsummated, engendering what H.D. calls the "fiery moment": "The perfection of the fiery moment can not be sustained—or can it?"[8] This recalls—and she quotes it—the Poundian

Le Paradis n'est pas artificiel
              but is jagged,

For a flash,
>> *for an hour.*
Then agony,
>> *then an hour,*
>>>> *then agony . . .*[9]

If this "fiery moment can not be sustained," for H.D. it became an enduring source of inspiration: "It filled my fantasies and dreams, my prose and poetry for ten years."[10] The youthful Pound becomes the *puer* in a reversed version of the Propertian "Ingenium nobis ipsa puella fecit" (My genius is no more than a girl), a phrase that echoes through Pound's own work. Paradoxically, it is the frustration of their love which creates its endurance as a source for poetry. "A sort of *rigor mortis* drove me onward. No, my poetry was not dead but it was built on or around the crater of an extinct volcano. Not *rigor mortis*. No, No! The vines grow more abundantly on those volcanic slopes. Ezra would have destroyed me and the center they call 'Air and Crystal' of my poetry."[11] Psychologically, this is perhaps not paradoxical at all; satiation engenders sleep rather than poetry. Pound, as we will see when we come to discuss his "Psychology and Troubadours," would later insist on the importance of "delay" in erotic encounters, as stimulative of the "psychic function."[12]

H.D.'s post facto comments on the events of her green time in Pennsylvania are, of course, reconstructions which necessarily have undergone a transformation in the mind of the mature poet. *End to Torment* is not, despite H.D.'s protestations about probable critical response, "naif."[13] Nothing makes this more apparent than a perusal of Pound's "Hilda's Book,"[14] written at the time of the events H.D. is remembering. Compared to *End to Torment*, "Hilda's Book" is stumbling indeed. Pound's inability to render his experience in any but the most conventional Rossettian terms is painfully apparent. But H.D. doesn't exactly "render" her experience either; she names it "the fiery moment." What is important for us is what she makes of this "fiery moment," not only as a source of creativity but as a subject for poetry. As late as 1959, H.D. was writing about her relationship with Ezra, in the poem "Winter Love" (in *Hermetic Definition*). In it, their relationship is transformed into myth, the personal basis abandoned in favor of universal statement. In *End to Torment* she gives us both the personal and the mythic.

H.D. clearly thinks that there is a personal dimension to Pound's work as well. She thinks that the "fiery moment" became a *subject* of his poetry as it did in hers. While the "reconstructed" nature of her account vitiates its evidential value to a degree, it is the best evidence we are likely to get about their youthful romance, because, as H.D. explains, the early letters from Pound were destroyed.

I don't suppose that I really wanted to keep his letters. There was a great untidy bundle of them, many of them written on notepaper he had appropriated from hotels, on a sort of grand tour a wealthy aunt or family friend had taken him. . . . I did not ask about the letters when I met my parents in Genoa, autumn 1912—was it? But my mother took me aside, "I think you will be relieved to know that your father burnt the old letters. . . ."[15]

Although we will never know just what was in Pound's letters that made it a "relief" to burn them, there must have been something there which to her parents' ears sounded "hot," perhaps to H.D.'s as well. If nothing else, those letters in the fire provide a good index of the *moeurs contemporaines* in the milieu Pound was just leaving, which in turn help to explain both the cryptic nature of some of his statements on the role of sexuality and the belligerent crudity of some of the others.

It would be presumptuous to catalogue H.D.'s comments on *The Cantos* which seem to bear on the "fiery moment," because to do so would be to reduce the range of resonance her remarks have within the "memoir" itself. Seemingly every comment has personal and mythic analogues somewhere in the book: "ply over ply." H.D. tends to understand the personal in terms of the mythic, and the mythic in terms of the personal. She refuses to reduce her experience in either direction, and her readers must follow her in this if they want to appreciate the text in its full integrity. With the critical pitfalls in mind, then, we can quote H.D. on Ezra and the felines:

We were curled up together in an armchair when my father found us. I was "gone." I wasn't there. I disentangled myself. I stood up; Ezra stood beside me. It seems we must have swayed, trembling. But I don't think we did. "Mr. Pound, I don't say there was any-thing wrong. . . . ." Mr. Pound, it was all wrong. You turn into a Satyr, a Lynx, and the girl in your arms (Dryad, you called her), for all her fragile, not yet lost virginity, is Maenad, bassarid. God keep us from Canto LXXIX, one of the Pisan Cantos.

Mr. Pound, with your magic, your "strange spells of old deity," why didn't you complete the metamorphosis? Pad, pad, pad, . . . come along, my Lynx.[16]

Of course, it's not only in the Lynx Canto that cats appear in *The Cantos;* they are part of an "ideogram" that appears often. What H.D.'s comments suggest, and what is implicit in Pound's work as a whole, is that Pound's cats are not only "hieratic," but signal a "metamorphosis" arising out of an erotic encounter as well. That the statement of this "metamorphic moment" should be so veiled is consistent with Pound's view of the myth-making process, as formulated in *The Spirit of Romance* (SR, 92).

Consider the following passage from Canto 79, which H.D. singles out for elaboration:

This fruit has a fire within it,
      Pomona, Pomona
No glass is clearer than are the globes of this flame
what sea is clearer than the pomegranate body
      holding the flame? [79/490]

She says of it, "There is no argument, pro or con. You catch fire or you don't catch fire."[17] This corresponds to Pound's frequent "those who have ears," but the passage she quotes also suggests "the fiery moment": "body holding the flame." This, too, is part of the Poundian ideogram for the erotic medium, things being lit from within, Scotus Erigena's "Omnia, quae sunt, lumina sunt." In his prose Pound would wait until his "Cavalcanti" essay to deal with this subject at any length, but it is there in the poetry from the beginning. For H.D., the state of mind which induced such a vision of things was invested with tremendous significance, as the following passage suggests:

Erich brought me a beautiful ruby-glass bowl from Venice. It is exactly Pomona, Pomona. "No glass is clearer than are the globes of this flame." I had not read this pomegranate section to Erich but the small cup-bowl—"no, no, not an ash-tray," I tell him— exactly materializes these lines. "This fruit has a fire within it." The small bowl is heavy with a white-blue-silver rim, one feels that it is filled with red wine. It is. "It is the Grail," I tell Erich.[18]

H.D.'s *End to Torment* is an enormously suggestive book, but except for the few passages she cites from *The Cantos* it is not a book which takes us a long way in interpreting Pound's poetry. "Fiery moment" is ultimately just a name, a name she has invested with a great deal of feeling. It provides us with a good index of the affective charge their encounters had, without telling us much about the particular kind of experience they underwent. One could come away from *End to Torment* thinking that here is a great deal of noise about adolescent sexuality, though I believe that would be a mistake. There is something extraordinary here, though perhaps no more can be claimed for Pound's experiences with H.D. than that they provided the seed which would later grow into the tree. H.D., when she says of the young woman who was Pound's "spirit love" during his St. Elizabeths years, "Undine seems myself *then* [in Pennsylvania],"[19] acknowledges that she was filling a role, and that there were others, perhaps many others, who later stood in her place. In 1933 Pound wrote to Viola Baxter Jordan that years of his life and work had been devoted to the investigation of "up-lift," of specific kinds of sexuality, and that his interest in Provence reflected this general interest, because it was there that the subject had been properly understood.[20] This suggests that we are not really dependent on H.D.'s account, that Pound's own writings ought to bear witness to his thought. And they do, but the mode of statement, as we will see, is extremely elliptical. It also suggests a beginning, another beginning, Pound's most outspoken treatise on the subject of Provence: "Psychology and Troubadours." By 1916 Pound's thinking about the "psychic function" of sexuality had taken on sharp outlines; if it had ever been, it was no longer emotion alone. Pound became more than "le Byron de nos jours," as H.D. at one point called him;[21] for Pound sexuality stood at the threshold of the *mysterium*, though he saw clearly enough that for many it was a source only of dissipation. Those are the ones who stopped with Circe.

Servants of Amor: The Early Poetry

You may take this if you like cum grano.
Pound, "Psychology and Troubadours"

In a footnote to "Psychology and Troubadours,"[1] commenting on
a "recent lecture by Mr. Mead,"[2] Pound makes the curious assertion that "there would seem to be in the legend of Simon Magus
and Helen of Tyre a clearer prototype of 'chivalric love' than in
anything hereinafter discussed" (*SR*, 91). Unfortunately, Pound
seems never to have written down just what that "prototype" was;
or perhaps, in deference to the reticence about bald statement he
found in the "trobar clus" (troubadour closed composition), he
simply chose to remain silent on the point. Initially, it seemed to
be just another enigmatic footnote, but then I remembered having
seen Simon Magus and Helen of Tyre mentioned before, in
Charles Williams's short history of the church, *The Descent of the
Dove*.[3] There, in a discussion of the early church, Williams mentions a spiritual "method" aimed at calling forth an experience of
the Spirit. It was

*dangerous but dangerous with a kind of heavenly daring. There
grew up, it seems, in that young and ardent body an effort to-
wards a particular spiritual experiment of, say, the polarization of
the senses. Our knowledge of it is very small, and is indeed confined to a famous passage of St. Paul, to a letter of St. Cyprian's,
and to one or two disapproving Canons of various Councils. The
method was probably not confined to the Church; it is likely to
have existed in other Mysteries. The great necromancer Simon*

Magus carried with him on his wanderings a companion who may have been for that purpose, and there were attributed to her high titles.[4]

Including, it seems, Helen of Tyre. There is something very Poundian about Williams's going on so about this as yet unspecified method of the "polarization of the senses," for which purpose Simon Magus perhaps carried about Helen of Tyre. We learn shortly that the method, as practiced within the church, did not involve a breach of Christian morality: "This is clear from that passage in St. Paul [still unspecified!] which shows that in some instances the experiment broke down owing to the sexual element between the man and the woman becoming too pronounced."[5] And finally, somewhat later, we find out what he is talking about: "The women—*subintroductae* as they were called—apparently slept with their companions without intercourse."[6]

I then remembered another enigmatic statement in "Psychology and Troubadours": "I have no particular conclusion to impose upon the reader; for a due consideration of Provençal poetry in 'trobar clus,' I can only suggest the evidence and lines of inquiry. The Pauline position on wedlock is of importance—I do not mean its general and inimical disapproval, but its more specific utterances" (SR, 95). The passage which both Williams and Pound seem intent to gesture at but not cite, is to be found in Paul's so-called advice to virgins (1 Corinthians 7.25–38, especially 36–38). It is not particularly suggestive; the King James version reads:

But if any man think that he behaveth himself uncomely toward his virgin, if she pass the flower of her age, and need so require, let him do what he will, he sinneth not: let them marry.

Nevertheless he that standeth stedfast in his heart, having no necessity, but hath power over his own will, and hath so decreed in his heart that he will keep his virgin, doeth well.

So then he that giveth her in marriage doeth well; but he that giveth her not in marriage doeth better.

If the evidence here seems almost nonexistent to the lay reader, Williams's and Pound's position is not beyond the bounds of the scholarly interpretation of the passage. While I don't want to enter the debate here, it is perhaps appropriate to note that *Peake's* Bible commentary lists as one of three possible glosses: "The custom of *virgines subintroductae* may have arisen early and this would explain the reference to virgins here. . . . Before monasteries and nunneries were built, the custom was common; bishops fulminated and councils legislated against it as it was open to scandal."[7] The question is not whether it ever existed, but if it existed so early within the church. Pound, apparently, thought it did.

One returns to "Psychology and Troubadours," after this short excursion, with a clearer sense of the locus in which Pound's comments there are to be understood. Baldly, sexual dalliance, of one sort or another, has been for certain individuals the source of contact with, for want of a better term, a visionary reality. While the details of this experiment remain, perhaps properly, veiled, it should be obvious that modern romantic effusions about the simple act are not indicated. Pound himself lampooned such drivel in his "Fratres Minores," noting that "the twitching of three abdominal nerves / Is incapable of producing a lasting Nirvana."[8] What we have instead is a sublimation, in the erotic encounter, of the lover's heightened sensitivity, Williams's "polarization of the senses."

Whether or not the "best modern scholarship" is willing to see a resurgence of this experiment in Provence is beyond the scope of our enquiry; what is pertinent is that Pound thought he did. Once we have circumscribed this locus, "Psychology and Troubadours" admits of only one reading: the essay is laced with cryptic references to the role of sexuality in the psychology of the troubadours; indeed, it would seem to be at the very basis of the psychology of the "servants of Amor." The temptation is to summarize the whole lot, but perhaps a couple of illustrations will suffice. Consider the following, peculiarly Poundian, "scientific" figure.[9]

Sex is, that is to say, of a double function and purpose, reproductive and educational; or, as we see in the realm of fluid force, one sort of vibration produces at different intensities, heat and light.

No scientist would be so stupid as to affirm that heat produced light, and it is into a similar sort of false ratiocination that those writers fall who find the source of illumination, or of religious experience, centered solely in the philo-progenitive instinct. [SR, 94]

About three pages later Pound returns to the same figure:

The electric current gives light where it meets resistance. I suggest that the living conditions of Provence gave the necessary restraint, produced the tension sufficient for the results, a tension unattainable under, let us say, the living conditions of imperial Rome.

So far as "morals" go, or at least a moral code in the modern sense, which might interfere in art, Arnaut can no more be accused of having one than can Ovid. Yet the attitude of the Latin doctor amoris *and that of the* gran maestro de amor *are notably different, as for instance on such a matter as delay. Ovid takes no account of the psychic function.* [SR, 97]

It is worth noting that Pound has circumscribed his subject in a rather careful manner: sexual experience is not the source of illumination but one source, nor is this just any sexual encounter, but one characterized by restraint, delay, and tension. And these, I think we must infer, are necessary rather than sufficient conditions for the success of the experiment. Furthermore, running throughout the essay is an emphasis on the character of the lover, who must have "a particular consitution of nerves and intellect."

At one point, Pound states, "The problem, in so far as it concerns Provence, is simply this: Did this 'chivalric love,' this exotic, take on mediumistic properties?" (SR, 94). It is, I think, basically a rhetorical question, except, perhaps, as it applies particularly to Provence; he had already stated, in a footnote on Cavalcanti, "For effect upon the air, upon the soul, etc., the 'lady in Tuscan poetry' has assumed all the properties of the Alchemist's stone" (SR, 90). What is particularly suggestive is that after a series of similar questions, he simply states, "For our basis in nature we rest on the indisputable and very scientific fact [Pound!] that there are in the 'normal course of things' certain times, a certain sort of moment more than another, when a man feels his immortality upon him" (SR, 94). It's the Poundian call to the experiential ground—we are to expect such experiences because they occur in "the natural course of events" (SR, 97). Furthermore, after a thumbnail sketch of those drawn to ecstatic cults, Pound announces, "One must consider that the types which joined these cults survived, in Provence, and survive, today—priests, maenads and the rest—though there is in our society no provision for them" (SR, 95). That such types survived in Provence, for the purposes of "Psychology and Troubadours," is relevant; that they survive today, is, in the immediate context, a superfluous and therefore significant observation. Perhaps Pound was merely extending the logic of his argument to its natural conclusion, but in light of his own early poetry, it seems more likely that he was looking toward his own life and work.[10]

Almost twenty years later, in "Terra Italica," we find Pound still writing around the question of the educative aspect of sexuality for men of a certain temperament, culminating perhaps in the single, trenchant phrase "For certain people the *pecten cteis* is the gate of wisdom" (cognates, the one Latin, the other Greek, each a euphemism for the genitalia).[11]

'Tis not a game that plays at mates and mating,
Provençe knew;
'Tis not a game of barter, lands and houses,
Provençe knew. [P, 50]

"Psychology and Troubadours" goes a long way toward clarifying the referent of the "it" (characteristically submerged in " 'tis") in these lines from "The Flame"; however, the sexual context here is rather broadly indicated in the first "is not" which clearly refers to the "reproductive" function. That the "educative" function is also present in "The Flame" is not so obvious. Pound, in his poetry as in his prose, addresses this matter with considerable circumspection. What we do get, rather than a direct statement about the circumstances, is a presentation of the substance of the visions beheld by the "servants of Amor," and an affirmation that it is one of those moments when the lover "feels his immortality upon him" ("our immortal moments" in "The Flame"). As for the vision,

There is the subtler music, the clear light
Where time burns back about th'eternal embers.
We are not shut from all the thousand heavens:
Lo, there are many gods whom we have seen,
Folk of unearthly fashion, places splendid,
Bulwarks of beryl and of chrysoprase. [P, 50]

The education is not so much a matter of refining one's sensibilities, though that too is indicated, as it is an education in the experience of visionary realities, and the accent falls on experience rather than knowledge. "If a certain number of people in Provence developed their own unofficial mysticism, basing it for the most part on *their own experience,* if the servants of Amor saw visions quite as well as the servants of the Roman ecclesiastical hierarchy . . . this may well have caused some scandal and jealousy to the orthodox" (SR, 91, my emphasis) (for Pound, the Albigensian Crusade, Montségur).

To understand "The Flame," and other early Pound poems dealing with the same complex of ideas, it is important to focus on the fact that the lover's experience with the woman involves a "bust thru from quotidien into the 'divine or permanent world.' " In "Psychology and Troubadours" it's man feeling "his immortality upon him." Perhaps the last stanza of "The House of Splendour" provides the clearest exposition of what Pound is talking about:

Here am I come perforce my love of her,
Behold mine adoration
Maketh me clear, and there are powers in this
Which, played on by the virtues of her soul,
Break down the four-square walls of standing time. [P, 49]

While the lover's own adoration is the agent that clarifies his psyche, it is the contact with the beloved which ushers the lover into the "permanent world." The obvious danger is a sentimental or "romantic" response to such passages; we must not forget that

Pound thought that the lady in Tuscan poetry functioned as an alchemist's stone, had mediumistic properties, so we should not be
surprised to find the same concept in Pound's own poetry, remembering that Pound's attraction to Tuscan and Provençal poetry was
an elective affinity and reflects on his own predilections.

Furthermore, the language of the passage does not actually
encourage a romantic response. It has analytical resonance, and
conveys a sense of objectivity and precision. It recalls Pound's
translation of the nineteenth-century Italian poet Giacomo Leopardi in "Her Monument, The Image Cut Thereon" : "Infinite
things desired, lofty visions / 'Got on desirous thought by natural
virtue."[12] However, the sense of precision should not, I think, here
be seen as a function of Pound's style so much as his subject matter: "Some mystic or other speaks of the intellect as standing in
the same relation to the soul as do the senses to the mind; and beyond a certain border, surely we come to this place where the ecstasy is not a whirl or a madness of the senses, but a glow arising
from the exact nature of the perception" (SR, 91). If Pound is being precise, we should not infer that this emphasis on precision is
in any way contrary to the "mystical" aspect of the experience.
Fuzziness is another matter altogether.[13]

If the virtues of the beloved's soul serve as a catalyst to "bust"
the lover into the permanent world, that is not to say there is any
necessity that the beloved too be transported into a visionary realm
by the experience. Indeed, in the last stanza of "The Flame,"
Pound seems to suggest that she isn't. The lover, rapt in his mystery, says:

Search not my lips, O Love, let go my hands,
This thing that moves as man is no more mortal.
If thou hast seen my shade sans character,
If thou hast seen that mirror of all moments,
That glass to all things that o'ershadow it,
Call not that mirror me, for I have slipped
Your grasp, I have eluded. [P, 51]

This is really rather peculiar, not so much in the estrangement of
the lover and the beloved at the moment of vision, which almost

has a logical necessity about it, but in the manifest lack of affection in "I have slipped your grasp," as if the beloved were a snare. However, I don't think this is a measure of the lover's disaffection, but rather a measure of the degree to which he is abstracted from quotidian realities—even the body has become a kind of poorly fitting garment, which Pound characterizes as "this thing."[14] But if "The Flame" ends on a note of estrangement, "The Summons" imagines a reciprocal education, each leading the other onward:

> *But as I am ever swept upward*
> *To the centre of all truth*
> *So must I bear thee with me*
> *Rapt into this great involving flame,*
> *Calling ever from the midst thereof,*
> > *"Follow! Follow!"*
>
> .   .   .   .   .
>
> *And together in the midst of this power*
> *Must we, each outstriving each,*
> *Cry eternally:*
> > *"I come, go thou yet further."*
> *And again, "Follow,"*
> *For we may not tarry.*[15]

The record seems to supply contradictory evidence, but perhaps this is simply a function of the experiential situation: that the beloved might or might not be rapt in the "great involving flame."

A great deal has been made of Pound's use of flowers as a kind of "erotic floral symbolism," for instance, and most famously, in "Coitus":

> *The gilded phaloi of the crocuses*
> > *are thrusting at the spring air.*
> *Here is there naught of dead gods*
> *But a procession of festival,*
> *A procession, O Giulio Romano,*
> *Fit for your spirit to dwell in.* [P, 110]

How those thrusting crocuses suggest those gilded "phaloi," very satisfying for the Freudian sensibility! (And Pound's sexuality has attracted a good deal of attention from Lacanian critics.)[16] But, for a Freudian, those next lines must be a little surprising, not to say incomprehensible. However, if one assumes the psychology of "Psychology and Troubadours" rather than the psychology of Freud, the transition is clear. The sexual encounter occasions vision, and here the vision is of a procession of the gods. Pound, of course, isn't explicit; he introduces the gods by the backhanded "naught of dead gods," leaving it to us to draw our conclusions. Presumably Giulio Romano serves as a shorthand notation for the style of the vision, and Ruthven's gloss on the passage is perhaps remotely appropriate to the case: "he [Giulio] painted mythological scenes as though they were something he had experienced and not merely read about: in his art the pagan gods live on" (a sentiment which is certainly consistent with Pound's thinking if we delete "as though").[17] In any case, in this poem, as in "The Flame," Pound plainly suggests that the locus of the vision is a sexual encounter. He is not always so straightforward.

Sometimes, indeed, Pound simply suppresses the situation altogether, and gives us a kind of cryptogram of the visionary moment. All we are really left to base our guesses on is the language, and the sphinxlike surface of the poem. "Heather," I think, falls into this class.

The black panther treads at my side,
And above my fingers
There float the petal-like flames.

The milk-white girls
Unbend from the holly-trees,
And their snow-white leopard
Watches to follow our trace. [P, 109]

Consider the dreamlike or visionary atmosphere of the poem, the use of words like petal, flame, and trace,[18] and the opposition of the black panther and the snow-white leopard, recalling Pound's comment that "at any rate, when we do get into contemplation of the flowing [Pound's universe of fluid force] we find sex, or some correspondance to it, 'positive and negative,' 'North and South,' 'sun and moon,' or whatever terms of whatever cult or science you

prefer to substitute" (*SR*, 93). That the panther and the leopard
are to correspond to the polarities of a man and a woman in a sexual encounter must, of course, barring some external evidence, remain speculative. But that Pound was capable of transforming an
experience to this degree to get it into a poem is demonstrable:
one need only compare "Shallott" and the prose note following it
in the *San Travoso Notebook*, where the poem is said to have been
inspired by the "essences of beauty" seen in the colors of the
dawn's "reflexion" (*CEP*, 327). In the poem, however, the Lord
of Shallott, prince of dreams, speaks and mentions neither the
dawn nor its colors. One would not want to push the point too
hard; "Heather" is cryptic in the extreme.

About midway between poems which clearly embody a sexual
encounter and an attendant visionary moment, such as "The
Flame," and suggestive utterances like "Heather," there are poems
like "Canzone: Of Angels," which exhibit the same configuration
of a visionary reality, a lady, and a man feeling his immortality
upon him—but with the sexual locus seemingly suppressed. "Canzone: Of Angels" begins familiarly enough:

He that is Lord of all the realms of light
Hath unto me from His magnificence
Granted such vision as hath wrought my joy.
Moving my spirit past the last defence
That shieldeth mortal things from mightier sight,
Where freedom of the soul knows no alloy,
I saw what forms the lordly powers employ. [*CEP*, 139]

There follows an extended description of the "similitude" of the
three splendors employed by the lordly powers which the speaker
has seen in vision. What comes after is one of the most interesting
passages in all of the early poems:

The diver at Sorrento from beneath
The vitreous indigo, who swiftly riseth,
By will and not by action as it seemeth,
Moves not more smoothly, and no thought surmiseth
How she takes motion from the lustrous sheath

Which, as the trace behind the swimmer, gleameth
Yet presseth back the aether where it streameth.
To her whom it adorns this sheath imparteth
The living motion from the light surrounding;
And thus my nobler parts, to grief's confounding,
Impart into my heart a peace which starteth
From one round whom a graciousness is cast
Which clingeth in the air where she hath past. [CEP, 140]

The language, of course, is hopelessly archaic, which probably accounts for the omission of the poem from *Personae*; but the figure is wonderful, and I think it is one of Pound's first successful attempts to embody the "radiant world," or as he variously calls it, the "universe of fluid force." The attempt for Pound is in the way of a recovery, because, as he says, "We appear to have lost the radiant world where one thought cuts through another with clean edge, a world of moving energies '*mezzo oscuro rade*', '*risplende in sè perpetuale effecto*', magnetisms that take form, that are seen, or that border the visible."[19] The recovery, however, is always possible in a world which has a "permanent basis in humanity." The radiant world is there and available to perception, "We are not shut from all the thousand heavens."

We should remember that Pound's ultimate interest is not in the lady herself but in the visionary reality she makes available. To put it crudely, she functions as a "mantram" or analogue of the alchemist's stone; she is a means to an end. Pound's early poetry does not suggest that he thought the sexual encounter was the sole means of approach. For instance, it is not by chance that Pound mentions as an example of "magnetisms that take form" in the radiant world "the form that seems a form seen in the mirror" (*LE*, 154). As early as *A Lume Spento* he had reported, in "On His Own Face in a Glass," that he saw not one face but a "myriad," a "ribald company," a "saintly host" (*CEP*, 34). We miss the point entirely if we read this as some kind of metaphor for a multifaceted personality; here too Pound speaks directly from experience. He sees many faces in the mirror; they are forms seen in the radiant world. What we have is another method of recovering the

radiant world, which we "appear" to have lost, another "experiment." Pound's commentary on Cavalcanti is again instructive; he
finds in Guido "*natural demonstration* and the proof by experience or (?) experiment" (*LE*, 158).

In "Canzone: Of Angels," the quality of the movement of the
diver at Sorrento figures the visionary movement of the beloved.
The pattern of the movement is the same, and the diver in the
vitreous indigo embodies that movement within the sensible world
(of "normal" experience). While the beloved's movement in the
realm of fluid force is something which is difficult for the uniniti-
ated to imagine, we can feel our way toward that perception by
"meditating" (Pound out of Richard of St. Victor) on the pattern
which is manifest in the diver's rise. The lover sees the beloved
move within a "lustrous sheath" which imparts motion from the
surrounding light (the radiant world).[20]

The obvious question is how does the lover's perception of the
beloved within the radiant world relate to the vision of the three
splendors which has preceded it? By now it should be clear that
the vision itself has sprung from the encounter of the lover with
the beloved, touched on in the lines "And thus my nobler parts, to
grief's confounding, / Impart into my heart a peace which starteth /
From one round whom a graciousness is cast." She is the source, or
the "mantram," of his vision.

Pound returns to the "ethereal sheath" in his well-known son-
net "A Virginal." In an elaboration of his experience of the beloved in the radiant world, the lover finds himself cloaked in a
"gauze of aether." For brevity's sake I quote the octet only:

No, no! Go from me. I have left her lately.
I will not spoil my sheath with lesser brightness,
For my surrounding air has a new lightness;
Slight are her arms, yet they have bound me straitly
And left me cloaked as with a gauze of aether;
As with sweet leaves; as with a subtle clearness.
Oh, I have picked up magic in her nearness
To sheathe me half in half the things that sheathe her. [CEP, 195]

The sexual encounter itself, indicated in the fourth line, has oc-
curred prior to the experience related in the poem. In this poem

Pound is writing about what the lover takes away from his contact with the beloved. The "new lightness" of the surrounding air is meant, perhaps, to figure the "special air" of the "pneumatici," which Pound thinks had an objective referent for Cavalcanti (*LE*, 177). Be that as it may, the very fact that Pound writes about the visionary encounter at a distance from the event suggests that he is writing from experience; and there are other poems which deal with the encounter at an even greater distance, placing the experience within the context of the lover's life. In this category are the poems "Horae Beatae Inscripto" and the very beautiful "Erat Hora":

"Thank you, whatever comes." And then she turned
And, as the ray of sun on hanging flowers
Fades when the wind hath lifted them aside,
Went swiftly from me. Nay, whatever comes
One hour was sunlit and the most high gods
May not make boast of any better thing
Than to have watched that hour as it passed. [P, 40]

A particularly enigmatic aspect of Pound's treatment of the visionary quality of the sexual encounter is hinted at in "Psychology and Troubadours" when he says of a poem by the Provençal poet Arnaut Daniel:

The crux of the matter might seem to rest on a very narrow base;
it might seem to be a matter of taste or of opinion, of scarcely
more than a personal predilection to ascribe or not to ascribe to
one passage in the canzon "Doutz brais e critz," a visionary signifi-
cance, where, in the third stanza, he speaks of a castle, a dream-
castle, or otherwise— as you like. [SR, 89]

If we turn to Pound's translation of this canzone we are, perhaps, truly baffled at the slenderness of the clue, for there is no mention of any "castle" whatever in the third stanza (*T*, 173).[21] However, in Pound's early poems, where we have been arguing the presence of visionary experience, there are many "dream" structures of just the sort he seems to be hinting inhabit Arnaut's canzone. For instance, in "Abelard," the third of the "Victorian Eclogues," Abelard prays:

Yea let thy angels walk, as I have seen
Them passing, or have seen their wings
Spread their pavilions o'er our twin delight. [CEP, 159]

Also in this class is the house of "The House of Splendour" ("A house not made with hands"), the golden house of "Apparuit," and this from "Sub Mare":

It is, and is not, I am sane enough,
Since you have come this place has hovered round me,
This fabrication built of autumn roses. [CEP, 194]

Or this, the second of the "Epigrams":

I looked and saw a sea
    roofed over with rainbows,
In the midst of each
    two lovers met and departed;
Then the sky was full of faces
    with gold glories behind them. [CEP, 151]

It should be obvious to the most casual reader that these structures receive some of the most ornate descriptions to be found in all of Pound's poetry; they are redolent with gold and roses, adorned with gems and wings, domed with rainbows. But besides their having, as Pound says, "a visionary significance," it is not at all clear what more can be said of them.

Pound, *in the middle* of his extended discussion of whether or not to ascribe visionary significance to Arnaut's dream-castle, *in the middle* of a very Poundian catalogue of both internal and external considerations (climate, temper, likely cultural influences), concedes "In none of these things singly is there any specific *proof*" (SR, 90). Of course, that "singly" is loaded, and another example of Pound's frequent and frustrating use of innuendo in place of bald statement. It suggests, I think, that together the items in his catalogue of considerations do amount to a kind of proof, while avoiding the responsibility of calling it a proof. It is this very aspect of Pound's style which makes writing on him a business of nuance, for if we demand from the record the kind of evidence on which we normally understand proofs to be based, it is impossible to *prove* whether or not Pound really intends us to understand that the sexual encounter, in these poems, is the occasion of a "bust" through into a visionary reality. But, like Pound in his study of Arnaut, while one can't marshal any specific proof, it is possible to discern in the accumulation of evidence, in the innuendos in the prose, in the linkage of a sexual locus to seemingly visionary events in the poems, and in the peculiar use of his visionary vocabulary in poems where the sexual locus seems to be present but suppressed, a kind of compelling pattern, which encourages our assent. We, too, must consider the temper of the time, Pound's sensibility, his emphasis on a "permanent basis in humanity," and statements like "I believe that Greek myth arose when someone having passed through delightful psychic experience tried *to communicate it to others and found it necessary to screen himself from persecution*" (SR, 92, my emphasis). In the background too is the sense of an elect, "those who have ears," who will understand a veiled statement as well as a bald, and as for those others who won't, Pound believes that "we have them always with us."

Pound's footnote on Mead's lecture on Simon Magus and Helen of Tyre has proved useful in unlocking a good number of Pound's early poems, poems which are, in essence, *poemes de clef.*[22] And while the text of Mead's lecture is unknown, his position on the significance of the relationship between Simon and Helen is evident in his earlier booklet *Simon Magus, An Essay*. It is emphatically not a position which Pound shared:

Now as the problem can be viewed from either the internal or external point of view, we have the mystery of the Soul depicted both from the side of the involution of spirit into matter and of the evolution of matter into spirit. If, on the one hand, we insist too strongly on one view, we shall only have a one-sided conception of the process; if, on the other, we neglect one factor, we shall never solve the at present unknown quantity of the equation. Thus the Soul is represented as the "lost sheep" struggling in the meshes of the net of matter, passing from body to body, and the Spirit is represented as descending, transforming itself through the spheres, in order to finally rescue its Syzygy from the bonds that are about her. . . . When this mystery is represented dramatically, so to say, and personified, these two aspects of the Soul are depicted as two persons. Thus we have Simon and Helen, his favourite disciple, Krishna and Arjuna, etc.[23]

Mead rejects the sexual locus altogether, reducing the record concerning the two to an allegory of the soul. The experiential element, stressed by Pound as a prototype of chivalric love, is singled out by Mead as a literalist reading propagated by hostile critics. But that is not to say that Mead actually denies the possibility that Simon himself may have fallen into a literalization; he suggests that the sources are too corrupt for us to be certain one way or another. But Mead is certain that if Simon read the tradition in this way he misread the tradition:

Naturally the language used is symbolical, and has naught to do with sex, in any sense. Woe unto him or her who takes these allegories of the Soul as literal histories, for nothing but sorrow will follow such materialization of divine mysteries. If Simon or his followers fell into this error, they worked their own downfall, under the Great Law, as surely as do all who forge such bonds of matter for their own enslavement.[24]

Whatever Mead's interpretation of the record, he did draw together an impressive compilation of source material concerning the careers, allegorical or otherwise, of Simon and Helen, as the first part of his booklet amply attests. We are left to assume that Mead introduced Pound to the history of the matter, but that Pound interpreted that history for himself, as Charles Williams did after him.

It seems to me that in point of temperament and belief Williams and Pound had very little in common, despite the shared link with T. S. Eliot. But, in any case, Pound would have very likely approved Williams's characterization of the suppression of this "questionable" experiment in the early church: "It was one of the earliest triumphs of 'the weaker brethren,' those innocent sheep who by mere volume of imbecility have trampled over many delicate and attractive flowers in Christendom."[25]

Divagation: Physiology

The study of physiognomy shd. be encouraged.
Pound, *Guide to Kulchur*

I turn now to a "divagation" from the more manifestly literary dimensions of Pound's visionary eroticism to what can only be
termed its physiological dimension. However, such a direction only
appears to be away from the literature, because Pound divulges in
his writings on physiology a good deal about his thinking that
bears forcefully, if obliquely, on the visionary side of his poetry.
There is something more here than a bizarre aside, however bizarre
an aside it may be. The primary texts for this diversion are Pound's
"Translator's Postscript" to Remy de Gourmont's *The Natural
Philosophy of Love*, certainly one of the most scandalous items in
the entire Pound bibliography, and his little-known review of Louis
Berman's *The Glands Regulating Personality*, "The New
Therapy."[1]

On the face of it, few of Pound's dicta seem less promising as
material for exegesis than his assertion in the "Translator's Postscript" that "it is more than likely that the brain itself, is, in origin
and development, only a sort of great clot of genital fluid held in
suspense or reserve" (NPL, 169). Stunned laughter is the obvious
response. Indeed, the tonalities of "great clot" and the postscript
as a whole suggest that Pound enjoyed composing it, but we
should not let the tone of the postscript or its disclaimers ("I appear to have thrown down bits of my note somewhat at random"
[NPL, 178]) interfere with our seeing that it is a careful piece of
writing and deserves a careful, exegetical reading.[2]

The title of the essay, "Translator's Postscript," insists on its relation to the "script" itself—Remy de Gourmont's *Physique de l'Amour*. The exact nature of the relation is difficult to determine, and finally, only tangential, though Pound accepted some of the strictures inherent in Gourmont's physiological perspective. In his *Lettres à l'Amazone*, Gourmont writes of love:

It is possible to describe love among the animals, including man considered as one of them, but human love cannot be described except by romantic outlines. It is possible to show it clearly in all those parts which are common to the whole of nature; but we cannot say clearly where it is different. We can study it systematically as an instinct, but not as a sentiment.[3]

From this angle the *Physique de l'Amour* is the possible essay on love, for the quotation describes its program: to set man down among the animals and describe the practices of love at that level. It's a tendentious book, despite the scientific trappings, tilted against sexual philistines and Darwinists.[4] The descriptions are sensuous, but unfortunately for the voyeurs who responded to the promising jackets of certain American editions, the effect is often, and sometimes intentionally, comic. For instance:

The mantis is almost the only insect with a neck; the head does not join the thorax immediately, the neck is long and flexible, bending in all directions. Thus, while the male is enlacing and fecundating her, the female will turn her head back and calmly eat her companion in pleasure. Here is one headless, another is gone up to the corsage, and his remains still clutch the female who is devouring him at both ends, getting from her spouse simultaneously the pleasures ac mensa ac thoro, *both bed and board from her husband.*[5]

Pound entered into the spirit of the work, not only in his translation, which is as light as the original and surprisingly literal, but in his postscript as well. He accepts, largely, the limits imposed by the "possible" essay on love. We are not left to infer this, Pound insists on it: "we are being extremely material and physical and animal, in the wake of our author" (*NPL*, 174).

The postscript is tangential to the script in that Pound's essay, while accepting the level of analysis suggested by Gourmont, actually only links up with it at a few points. Anyone who has read the entire *Physique de l'Amour* knows that the phrases Pound approves in the postscript are extraordinary in the book itself. None is more so, perhaps, than the one Pound takes as an epigraph: "Il y aurait peut-être une certain corrélation entre la copulation completè et profonde et le développement cérébral" ("There might be, perhaps, a certain correlation between complete and profound copulation and the development of the brain," in Pound's translation [*NPL*, 169]). In Gourmont, the passage caps a chapter on "love organs," and is a passing reflection on specifically physical questions of genital design in "mammifera and arthropoda" and their correlation with highly developed intelligence in the same two "great branchings." Pound takes the matter up; he will discuss the relation between "profound copulation" and "cerebration." Though really, in context, it would have been better, perhaps, to translate "profonde" simply as "deep."

Pound's postscript diverges from the *Physique* in other significant ways as well. For instance, while Gourmont by and large restricts the mode of his analysis to description of external behaviors and inferences drawn from them, Pound "introspects it" when he can, and speculates on the significance of these subjective data in terms of physiology (or a simulacrum thereof); it is only to this extent that he is "extremely material and physical and animal" in his analysis. Furthermore, it is a small but daring step from the development of cerebral capacity in a species to the development of cerebral capacity in an individual—a step Pound takes, and self-consciously. Pound espouses the Lamarckian view that changes in the species occur as changes in an individual, which are then "passed on." On the basis of an introspection, Pound argues that such mutations happen suddenly,

with a conviction for which anyone is at liberty to call me a lunatic, and for which I offer no better ground than simple introspection. I believe, and on no better ground than that of a sudden emotion, that the change of the species is not a slow matter, . . .

*I believe that the species changes as suddenly as a man makes a
song or a poem, or as suddenly as he starts making them.* [NPL, 174]

The iterated *credo* is telling. Despite the qualifications this is no
modest statement, because to know by introspection an advance in
the species one must be the individual to make it.

  With the site of Pound's enquiry determined, the postscript
seems less difficult, and we are better prepared to deal with the
notorious statement quoted at the beginning of the chapter, "it is
more than likely that the brain itself, is, in origin and development, only a sort of great clot of genital fluid held in suspense or
reserve." The meaning of this passage hinges on Pound's characterization of the genital fluid: "the power of the spermatozoid is
precisely the power of exteriorizing a form" (*NPL*, 169). Readers
of Pound's *Cantos* should be on familiar ground here, for this is
the power of the acorn to exteriorize the form of the oak: "oak
leaf never plane leaf" (87/573). The relationship of this phenom-
enon, of the seed to cast a form, to the functioning of the brain is,
presumably, an example of what Pound calls in the postscript "as
yet uncorrelated phenomena" (*NPL*, 169). The link, for Pound,
is that the brain functions in a like manner; it has an "enormous
content" as "a maker and presenter of images" (*NPL*, 169). That
the functions are analogous is clear, and it is in the realm of analo-
gies that Gourmont can speak, and Pound quotes him, of "fecundating a generation of bodies as genius fecundates a generation of
minds" (*NPL*, 173). But Pound is saying more than that; he is
asserting a physiological relation between the exteriorizing functions of the spermatozoid and the brain. At this the intuitive mind
balks, and demands a little coaching.[6]
  Pound makes a poor coach, offering instead a few red herrings
by way of explanation for what he thinks is the physiological basis
of the functional parallelism of the brain and sperm. At one point
he cites "the lack of any other known substance [besides sperm] in
nature capable of growing into brain" (*NPL*, 169) as evidence for
the relation, but the obvious objection "or into an arm" suggests
that this is an indirection. The real link is more introspective than

this, and is introduced clandestinely. It will be remembered that Gourmont's correlation of intelligence to "profonde" copulation was a matter of genital design, of the depth of penetration. Though Pound takes this correlation as his starting point, he never returns to it in its Gourmontian form; instead, he silently amends it to a correlation between intelligence and a specific kind of copulation, characterized in such terms as "suspense," "reserve," and "retention," a characterization that leads him to note that "A flood is as bad as a famine" (*NPL*, 170–71). Nothing here about design, because this is not Gourmont. Pound's version:

Species would have developed in accordance with, or their development would have been affected by the relative discharge and retention of the [spermatic] fluid; this proportion being both a matter of quantity and of quality, some animals profiting hardly at all by the alluvial Nile-flood; the baboon retaining nothing; men apparently stupefying themselves in some cases by excess, and in other cases discharging apparently only a surplus at high pressure; the imbecile, or the genius, the 'strongminded.' [*NPL*, 169]

The effect of "relative discharge and retention" remains constant; in species, those retaining nothing suffer an atrophy in their development, and vice versa; in man, it is a question of individuals: excess discharge possibly leading to imbecility, retention leading to strength of mind, even to genius (remembering the qualitative dimension that crosscuts the simply quantitative question). There is here, of course, a significant echo of Pound's assertions in "Psychology and Troubadours," where he insisted on the importance of "delay" in the sexual encounter, if it is to serve a "mediumistic" function in the psychic life of the lover (*SR*, 97). This suggests that the compact experience remains the same, but depending on the character of the work, Pound emphasizes one or another aspect of it. From every perspective, though, indulging in simple copulation is lampooned as an inferior approach to sexuality; here it is stupefaction by excess.

But if "delay" tells us something about the condition in which a physiological relation between the sperm and brain is best generated, the question of mechanism remains, in that there is no obvious conduit between the genitalia and the brain. It will be necessary to digress a little further before we can resolve this problem. Discussing sexual dimorphism, with respect to aptitudes, Pound posits for woman "hereditary aptitudes, better than the male in the 'useful gestures,' the perfections," for man "the 'inventions,' the new gestures, the extravagance, the wild shots, the impractical, merely because in him occurs the new up-jut, the new bathing of the cerebral tissues in the residuum, in *la mousse* of the life sap" (*NPL*, 170).[7] Although this reinforces our perception that Pound is talking about an actual rather than a metaphoric sexual encounter, the question of a conduit remains unresolved—just how does the residuum, the froth, the retained genital fluid, get from down there to up there?

Pound seems to be cognizant of the problem; later in the essay he provides a tentative, physiological answer, without, however, reminding us of the question. Apparently *la mousse* must be translated, by way of the glands, from the chemical to the electrical systems. The conduit is electrical:

People were long ignorant of the circulation of the blood; that known, they appeared to think the nerves stationary; Gourmont speaks of the "circulation nerveuse," but many people still consider the nerve as at most a telegraph wire, simply because it does not bleed visibly when cut. The current is "interrupted." The school books of twenty years ago were rather vague about lymph, and various glands still baffle physicians. I have not seen the suggestion that some of them may serve rather as fuses in an electric system, to prevent short circuits, or in some variant or allotropic form. [*NPL*, 178]

About the function of glands Pound would have more to say within the year, and this remark suggests that Pound was already nursing the idea that glands might play a more important part in the spectrum of erotic response than he was yet able to substantiate.[8] But, even more transparently, this passage looks back to "Psychology and Troubadours" where Pound asserted that an "electric current gives light where it meets resistance" (*SR*, 97), which we took to be metaphorical, but which is perhaps not only metaphorical. The status of electricity in Pound's thought is certainly not as mechanistic as it is in the "normal" account. In his "Cavalcanti" he asserted that

A medieval 'natural philosopher' would find this modern world full of enchantments, not only the light in the electric bulb, but the thought of the current hidden in air and in wire would give him a mind full of forms, 'Fuor di color' or having their hyper-colours. The medieval philosopher would probably have been unable to think the electric world, and not think of it as a world of forms. [LE, 154–55]

For Pound, electricity, both in the light bulb and in the body, is a subtle energy, an energy in "the radiant world." Pound's physics seems always entwined with his metaphysics.[9]

Although the conduit between the genitalia and the brain is nervous, electrical, Pound describes the transactions in terms of fluidity;[10] the cerebral tissues are "bathed." For this bathing Pound makes extravagant claims. Following Gourmont, Pound situates the human case in the larger context of the animal kingdom, from which it follows that the power to exteriorize a form, once attributed to "cerebral fluid," should be visible in nature's every compartment. To demonstrate this Pound takes up "four important branches" of nature, characterizing each branch "according to their apparent chief desire, or source of choosing their species. Insect, utility; bird, flight; mammal, muscular splendour; man, experiment" (NPL, 171). As science, this is cavalier in the extreme, but Pound's taking "experiment" as the "apparent chief desire" of the human species is instructive in light of his insisting on Cavalcanti's predilection for natural demonstration. However, if we simply accept the word experiment at face value we will find it difficult to comprehend Pound's thought, because Pound wants to extend or recover what he takes to be the proper range of subjects for experimentation. Consider the following: "In his growing subservience to, and adoration of, and entanglement in machines, in utility, man rounds the circle almost into insect life, the absence of flesh; and may have need even of horned gods to save him, or at least of a form of thought which permits them" (*NPL*, 172). Since machines are clearly the result of a certain kind of experiment, and Pound has taken experimentation as man's chief desire, this criticism of machines seems contradictory.

The resolution of this problem is to be found in the question of subject matter. Pound disapproves of the restriction of the range of experimental subjects to things "out there," to tools and to utility. "The invention of the first tool turned his [man's] mind (using this term in the full sense); turned, let us say, his 'brain' from his own body. No need for greater antennae, a fifth arm [one wonders about the third and fourth], etc., except, after a lapse, as a *tour de force*, to show that he is still lord of his own body" (*NPL*, 175). To make tools can exert a fascination on the mind which precludes further experimentation on man himself. It is from this turning away that we may need a "horned god" to save us, because Pound takes horned gods as an example, facetiously or not, of what man might make of himself if he were to take himself as subject:

Let us suppose man capable of exteriorizing a new organ, horn, halo, Eye of Horus. Given a brain of this power, comes the question what organ, and to what purpose?

Turning to folk-lore, we have Frazer on horned gods, we have Egyptian statues, generally supposed to be "symbols," of cat-headed and ibis-headed gods. Now in a primitive community, a man, a volontaire, might risk it. He might want prestige, authority, want them enough to grow a cat head; Greek philosophy would have smiled at him, would have deprecated his ostentation. [*NPL*, 176]

The danger in reading Pound is to read symbolically what is meant literally, but I am not sure Pound really expects us to see in the question of a horn more than an index of what a man might feel to be possible, "man feeling this protean capacity to grow a new organ" (*NPL*, 177). But Pound would not, after all, be the first poet in English to think it might be possible; Christopher Smart, in his *Jubilate Agno*, is not writing symbolically when he considers horns:

For I prophecy that we shall have our horns again.
For in the day of David Man as yet had a glorious
  horn upon his forehead.
For this horn was a bright substance in colour &
  consistence as the nail of the hand.
For it was broad, thick and strong so as to serve
  for defence as well as ornament.

.   .   .   .

For I prophecy that the English will recover their
  horns first.
For I prophecy that all nations of the world
  will do the like in turn.
For I prophecy that all Englishmen will wear their
  beards again.
For a beard is a good step to a horn.[11]

Pound, of course, wore a beard.

In the end, Pound dismisses horns in a summary manner, "you
have all sorts of aptitudes developed without external change,
which in an earlier biological state would possibly have found
carnal expression" (NPL, 176). Pound is not interested in growing
a horn; their introduction into the discusssion, however, serves two
functions in the progress of the essay. On the one hand, as mentioned previously, it provides a good index of the intensity of feeling Pound means us to understand when he discusses "man feeling this protean capacity"; on the other hand, it is, by normal standards, impossible. Pound's actual interest is in what faculties man
might develop or recall if he would redirect his power of invention
from the world to himself, a power Pound believed could be aug-
mented by a proper management of one's sexuality. In Pound's
discussion of faculties, as an alternative to "carnal expression," the
examples he gives are also by normal standards impossible: Saint
Teresa seeing the microcosmos, complete, " 'the size of a wal-
nut,' " and a London wool-broker visualizing the entire contents
of a 300-folio letter-file, "the size of two lumps of loaf sugar laid
flat side to flat side" (NPL, 177).[12] In the realm of faculties,
changes not requiring "carnal expression," Pound insists that com-

monsense conceptions regarding the possible are too restrictive. Man has not arrived at the end of his evolution: "Not considering the process ended; taking the individual genius as the man in whom the new access, the new superfluity of spermatozoic pressure (quantitative and qualitative) upshoots into the brain, alluvial Nile-flood, bringing new crops, new invention" (*NPL*, 179).[13] Simply put, Pound maintains that the right man, with a retention of sperm appropriate to his constitution, is capable of developing faculties normally considered impossible. Furthermore, in his insistence on the introspective mode of his analysis, Pound implies a preoccupation on his own part with the relation between his sexual activity and his mental faculties, states of mind.

Within the confines of an "extremely material" postscript there is not much room for a discussion of just what is to be done with this "protean capacity," particularly after Pound dispenses with material "en-fleshment" as an option: "Without then the ostentation of an organ." Pound leaves the "invention" to our imagination, his interest being, in the postscript, the condition favoring invention: "Given the spermatozoic thought, the two great seas of fecundative matter, the brain lobes, mutually magnetized, luminous in their knowledge of their being; whether they may be expected to seek exterior 'luxuria', or whether they are going to repeat Augustine hymns, is not in my jurisdiction" (*NPL*, 179). Pound's reticence on this point may stem, ultimately, from the fact that sexual activity, of any sort, has a normative dimension; it is clear that both Pound and Gourmont feel that the mores of their time are too restrictive, and they each make an oblique attack on them, enlisting the prestige of "science." Hence Pound's maintaining that the relation of sexual activity to creative thought "is a question of physiology, it is not a question of morals and sociology" (*NPL*, 179). Pound's perception that "natural demonstration," in sexual experiments, would likely have meant censure in 1922 is surely accurate and partially accounts, I think, for the convoluted structure of the essay. It is a subject Pound treats obliquely at best whenever he treats it.

But in terms of a state of mind, Pound's apperception of the brain lobes as "mutually magnetized, luminous in their own knowledge of their being" seems to have been synthesized with "the power to exteriorize a form," common to all *semen* (to the brain, sperm, and the acorn), to yield the "great acorn of light" of *The Cantos*. The apperceptual element in this cannot be overstressed, though this is not to deny that further levels of meaning can be separated out from the synthetic "great acorn of light." For instance, Sieburth argues that "the acorn (Latin *glans*) is a traditional sexual symbol and thus rejoins the 'spermatozoic' light ('bulging outward') of Pound's 'Postscript' to the *Physique de l'Amour*."[14] What must be fought against is the tendency of symbology to usurp experience, whence, "the 'great acorn of light' here may be taken as a dense emblem of Pound's *paradiso*."[15] Presentation, not representation.

Despite Remy de Gourmont's insisting to *l'Amazone* that human love can only be described where it coincides with love as it is found among the animals, in his oeuvre he attempted the impossible many times, indeed in *Lettres à l'Amazone* itself. Pound is fully aware of this, and sketches what he understands to be the Gourmontian reach along the continuum of Amor in his "Remy de Gourmont": "*Physique de L'Amour* (1903) should be used as a text-book of biology. Between this biological basis in instinct, and the 'Sequaire of Goddeschalk' in *Le Latin Mystique* (1892) stretch Gourmont's studies of amour and aesthetics" (*LE*, 343). If these are the end points, Pound places many other of Gourmont's works on the line that stretches between them in his "distinction." This subtitle is not gratuitous; just as Gourmont performed a series of distinctions on the compound "love," Pound is distinguishing between the various works of Gourmont. Pound does not assert that the end points of the Gourmontian range are the end points of the entire continuum of Amor, and, indeed, to assume that he does would be a grave obstacle to understanding Pound's own eroticism, which stretches from the chemical to the visionary. Pound insists on his own "dissociations"; of Gourmont, he says,

In a criticism of him, 'criticism' being an over-violent word, in, let us say, an indication of him, one wants merely to show that one has himself made certain dissociations; as here, between the aesthetic receptivity of tactile and magnetic values, of the perception of beauty in these relationships and the conception of love, passion, emotion as an intellectual instigation; such as Propertius claims it; such as we find declared in the King of Navarre's
      'De fine amor vient science et beauté';
and constantly in the troubadours. [LE, 343–44, *my emphasis*]

Pound, on the basis of his own researches, contrasts the eroticisms of Gourmont with the "Propertian attitude": "Ingenium nobis ipsa puella fecit" (my genius is no more than a girl). Eroticism as "intellectual instigation" is *a* Poundian attitude,[16] but only one among many, just as the "biological basis in instinct" explored by Gourmont in the *Physique* is Gourmontian but does not exhaust Gourmont's range. We, too, must perform "dissociations" on the eroticism of Pound, or we will be left with useless word magic like "phallic synthesis" to describe something we don't understand.

Pound closes the "Translator's Postscript" with a historical catalogue of approaches to eroticism as they bear on thought. It is instructive, if not complete. Unfortunately, the significance of individual items is left to our investigation.

It remains that man has for centuries nibbled at this idea of connection, intimate connection between his sperm and his cerebration, the ascetic has tried to withhold all his sperm, the lure, the ignis fatuus perhaps, of wanting to super-think; the dope-fiend has tried opium and every inferior to Bacchus, to get an extra kick out of the organ, the mystics have sought the gleam in the tavern, Helen of Tyre, priestess in the temple of Venus, in Indian temples, stray priestesses in the streets, unuprootable custom, and probably with a basis of sanity. A sense of balance might show that asceticism means either a drought or a crowding. The liquid solution must be kept at the right consistency; one would say the due proportion of liquid to viscous particles [sperm to brain], a good circulation [nervous]; the actual quality of the sieve or separator

*[person], counting perhaps most of all; the balance and retentive
media.*
     Perhaps the clue is in Propertius after all:
          Ingenium nobis ipsa puella fecit.
*There is the whole of the XIIth century love cult, and Dante's
metaphysics a little to one side, and Gourmont's Latin Mystique.*
[NPL, 180]

For clarity's sake I have made a few interpolations in one sentence; in light of the foregoing analysis their accuracy should be
apparent. For the postscript it is an important sentence, coming as
it does in the middle of the catalogue, because in it Pound insists
on a "biological basis" for every item. Interpreters of an allegorizing tendency should take note.
     The catalogue is probably not as accidental as it appears. In
the "Shop Girl" of *Lustra* Pound establishes his filiation to the
Propertian "intellectual instigation," though at a level of compac-
tion that allows him to include as instigators "stray priestesses in
the streets":

For a moment she rested against me
Like a swallow half blown to the wall,
And they talk of Swinburne's women,
And the shepherdess meeting with Guido.
And the harlots of Baudelaire. [P, 112][17]

Hugh Kenner's gloss on the poem is interesting but in light of this
analysis possibly skewed: "—another girl now remembered in absence, but never properly present: molecule of the merest encounter, 'like a swallow half blown to the wall': yet a muse as were the
women in other poets' perhaps imaginary encounters: and she was
real. And nearly non-existent: and granted no favors: and granted
the stuff of a tiny poem."[18] Pound's catalogue suggests, I think,
that we are not meant to doubt the reality of the other poets' encounters, that Pound thinks all the women were present enough
to facilitate a "good circulation." The accent is on presence, not
"near non-existence."
     Despite Pound's reticence about what he thinks might be a

good use of "spermatic thought" as a matter outside his jurisdiction, he does have his preferences. He doesn't follow Gourmont as far as "Ce qui est bon, c'est ce qui est, et qui est contient ce qui sera."[19] For Gourmont nothing is "CONTRA NATURAM." With respect to the catalogue, we will see that Pound derides ascetics and fornicators, and dope fiends, in the Lotophagoi Canto. Not every item in the catalogue, perhaps, can be explicated from this distance. For instance, "the mystics [who] have sought the gleam in the tavern" probably refers to the Omar Khayyam of FitzGerald's *Rubaiyat*, but it is difficult to tell what Pound thought of it. He approved of the poem, but at the same time realized it was a mistranslation (*LE*, 34).[20] The presence of the "XIIth century love cult" is, of course, immediately explicable in light of Pound's recital of the practices of the "servants of Amor." Dante's metaphysics is a "little to one side," one supposes, because the Beatrice who inspired it was by the time of its composition already dead, and it could only be her image, "dove sta memoria," rather than her physical self, which could serve as the alchemist's stone in calling forth vision. And, if we take "Gourmont's Latin Mystique" to be a reference to Godeschalk's "sequaire" (a safe assumption, I think), we find the tradition reentering the church, in the nuns who personalize Christ as a lover and thus create an image for their passion which in turn is sublimated. The erotic element is certainly pronounced: "Christ sleepeth with them: happy is this sleep, sweet the rest there, wherein true maid is fondled in the embraces of her heavenly spouse."[21] Here, as in Dante, there is not a real beloved; instead an image of the beloved is held in the mind. This is, then, related, but "to one side."

Pound's preoccupation with sexuality and its relation to thought did not begin with his translating the *Physique de l'Amour*. The "Hieratic Head of Ezra Pound," executed by his friend, the sculptor Henri Gaudier-Brzeska, was finished by 1914; the sculpture is overwhelmingly phallic. Kenner suggests that maybe the "Hieratic Head" "catalyzed" in Pound the ideas that found expression in the "Postscript." Perhaps, but it seems more likely that Pound in conversation suggested to Gaudier the "certain emotions"[22] which resulted in the sculpture. Furthermore, the sculpture is not only phallic, it is hieratic. This linking of the seminal and the spiritual is not gratuitous; it is the same linkage we observe in Pound's own thought, and not only after Gaudier sculpted the head, but before, as we have already demonstrated in Pound's "Psychology and Troubadours," an essay which also suggests the logic of Helen of Tyre's presence in the final catalogue of the "Translator's Postscript."

In 1921 the American physician Louis Berman published *The Glands Regulating Personality*; it was a book which attracted Pound's attention and excited his admiration.[23] In "The New Therapy,"[24] a *New Age* review, Pound gauged the significance of the book as "one of the great revolutions in medicine; a revolution as great as that caused by Pasteur,"[25] and asserted that it offered "a comforting relief from Freudian excess."[26] If Berman's name hasn't eclipsed Freud's and Pasteur's in the public mind, his book has seen a second, revised edition (1928) and a recent reprinting (1970). But Berman's impact is not really in question here; it is more important to understand why Pound was so enthusiastic about the work and what aspects of Berman's analysis Pound found the most significant.

The Glands Regulating Personality, as Pound realized, is a work of popular science, aimed principally at the general reader. It abounds in literary allusions and, for a medical treatise, is written with considerable verve. But even in this age of naive reductionist accounts of human behavior, Berman's book seems naively reductionist in tenor. Berman takes "glandular inheritance" as *the* determining factor in the development and performance of the individual and ignores every other possible influence: nutrition, environment, education, and so forth. "Glandular inheritance" is simply the determinant given, and is always considered as a constant. That glands might be susceptible to stimulation, an idea which would have appealed to the Pound of "Psychology and Troubadours," is simply not considered. Experiments designed to demonstrate the influence of specific glands always involve glandular failure or the introduction of the gland externally (by ingestion or implantation). If Pound is troubled by the primitiveness of the methodology or the reductionist tilt of the book, it is not apparent in his review, which, perhaps for tendentious reasons, is positive if a little indulgent.

On the most general level, Berman's recital of the function of glands in "regulating" personality provides Pound with another piece of evidence for his attack on those dualists who want to see the mind and the body as separate entities, and usually to see the body as evil. Pound here continues to champion what he calls elsewhere "Mediterranean sanity" (*LE*, 154 et circa) against the evils of asceticism, the Albigensians against the "testy" monks. For Pound, the body is a "perfect instrument of the increasing intelligence" (*LE*, 152), and not an obstruction to that intelligence. The body is not something to be gotten over; it is something to be cultivated.

But if this is Pound's general position, the focus of his review of Berman's *Glands Regulating Personality* reveals a more particular interest. Structurally, the review in its relation to Berman's book is very much like the relation of the "Postscript" to Remy de Gourmont's *Physique de l'Amour*; it maintains the same level of analysis (glandular) but moves substantively at a tangent. The direction of the tangent reveals Pound's interest. He is taking up where the "Postscript" left off, refining his speculations. Pound doesn't leave it to the reader to think of Gourmont's *Physique*; he insists on its relation to the review, twice mentioning the book. In the "Postscript," Pound, in grappling with the problem of a conduit between the genitalia and the brain, suggested that glands might have a role in the "circulation nerveuse," that in the electrical conduit they might "serve rather as fuses in an electric system, to prevent short circuits, or in some variant or allotropic form" (*NPL*, 178). Apparently Pound pursued the question; how else can we explain a book like Berman's finding its way into his hands? It would make a very suspicious accident.

Pound was not, perhaps, fully confirmed in his expectations. The problem turned out to be a little more complicated than he had imagined. But then, it is very difficult "to introspect" glandular functions. In "The New Therapy" Pound wants to reevaluate the position he took in the "Postscript." He writes, "I postulated a double secretion of the gonads, or at least spoke of them as a sieve. I made various statements now antiquated, and indulged in some speculations as yet neither supported nor disproved."[27] Pound, in perusing *Glands Regulating Personality*, found his earlier assumption that the gonads would be the natural glands implicated in a discussion of the relation of sexuality to "cerebration" too narrow, too exclusively gonadal, so to speak. In a table of eight endocrines, which Pound redacts out of Berman, five are explicitly related to sexuality in their functioning.[28] Rather than a "double secretion" of the gonads there is a consort of glands acting in conjunction with one another. What remains the same is that the glands are seen to bear on consciousness: "when the secretions of these glands interact in certain ways, they produce definite chemical pressure, and when this pressure reaches a certain intensity it forces itself on the consciousness."[29] There are certain peculiarities in the language of this passage, further establishing a link between "The New Therapy" and both the "Postscript" and ultimately "Psychology and Troubadours." The phrase "chemical pressure," picked up from Berman, must have suggested to Pound the experience which led him to emphasize pressure and restraint in his previous discussions of sexuality: the role of delay in the sublimation of sexual desire into vision.

There is a further link with the two earlier essays in the question of personality types. I have already cited, in the chapter devoted to "Psychology and Troubadours," Pound's assertion that the types of people who joined ecstatic cults in Greece survived in Provence and still survive (*SR*, 95). In the "Postscript" the question of types is implicit in Pound's assertion that "the actual quality of the sieve or separator" counts "perhaps most of all" (*NPL*, 180). In "The New Therapy" and in Berman's book, personalities are typed according to glandular dominance. Pound realizes that this schema invites misuse, and lampoons it, albeit gently: "long-suffering humanity [is divided] into a new set of types (interest for all dilletante palmists, astrologers, character-readers, etc.)."[30] But he must feel that there is a real basis for distinction, because he adopts Berman's typology for the rest of his review.

Berman's own system compasses several types; *his* interest is in the function of glands in general. Pound's interest, for tendentious reasons, is restricted to the pineal and pituitary glands. I think it will be best to quote Pound's remarkable ideas at length, remembering that he is "putting together my earlier speculations [those of the "Postscript"] and Berman's data."[31] The paragraphing is Pound's:

The pineal . . . contains two things, cells filled with a pigment like that in the eye's retina, and little piles of lime salt crystals (which resist the action of X-rays). I suggest that the pineal is not an extinct eye, that Descartes had some ground for his belief in its being the seat of some activity almost important enough to be called "the soul." In tabular form:

> *Pineal: gland of "lucidity," of the sense of light analogous to the eye, perhaps as the fibres of Corti in the ear show analogy to stringed instrument. gland of metamorphosis, of original thought, the secretion being very probably just the lime salts crystals well known to lie in it, but they may be secreted not as a slow effusion, but ejected suddenly into sensitized area, analogy to the testes. This causes the new juxtaposition of images. The original thought, as distinct from imitative thought.*

> *Light, or the sensation of light, may well be the combustion or encounter of this retina-pigment either, as in the eye, with exterior vibrations, or in the pineal with the emanation of brain cells, or even with the cells themselves.*

> *Berman postulates the posterior pituitary as the gland of hallucination. I want to distinguish between the orderly visualization which I presume to be pineal, but which neither confuses nor annoys the visionary, and D.T.'s, or any other sort of hallucination. It is possible that the activity of the pineal may be limited to controlling the post-pituitary phantasma. . . .*

> *Contrast of Pineal with Pituitary: very possibly that the Pineal represents intelligence developed from sight; the pituitary, intelligence from smell, the keen-scent, hot on the trail type. In attributing the Pineal to adolescence, Berman may take an effect for a cause. The Pineal does usually decline after adolescence, but so also does the faculty for physical growth, and the general adaptability of the animal.*

Summarising again:
Pineal: secretion? retinal pigment lime salt in
> *crystal form.*
> *function: sense of vision, sense of light flowing*
> *along the nerves and making one aware where one's*
> *hands are in the dark.*
> *luminosity in vision, "gates of beryl and*
> *chrysoprase" effect, power of visualization as*
> *distinct from hallucination.*
> *Intelligence developed from seeing, telescopic as*
> *opposed to telepathic intelligence.*
> *Pituitary: intelligence developed from smell.*[32]

Within the range of glandular regulation Pound has chosen to focus on the possible effect of the pineal and pituitary glands on consciousness, specifically on experiences designated as "visionary" and "hallucinatory." If this focus is narrow and suggestive, the subject is not a new one for Pound, excepting the glandular context. Previously, in a draft of an "Ur-Canto," Pound had struggled to distinguish in his own life between vision and hallucination, in a world where hallucination had largely if not completely usurped the place of vision, where "the seeing of visions" was no longer "considered respectable" (SR, 105).

> *But your visions,*
> *Your finest visions are half from fever,*
> *you've admitted it.*
> *//////////// ////////////*
> *No that I haven't*
> *I've seen gold once. with a liver,*
> *But other times when I was in perfect health,*
> *No . more than half of them when I was hale,*
> *afoot upon the roads. hearty with walking.*
> *I'll not tie all thought upon my nether vitals.*[33]

By attributing vision to pineal influence, and hallucination to pituitary, Pound perhaps hoped to drive a conceptual wedge (indeed a physiological wedge, to strain a metaphor) between the two kinds of experiences. It is a dissociation in the Gourmontian tradition. But to call the one pineal and the other pituitary is of little pragmatic use for the subject of a questionable experience, for the Pound of the "Ur-Canto" just cited. It does, however, suggest that there is a distinction to be made, which is an important contribution to understanding Pound's attempts to come to grips with his experiences in an age that lumps the matter under one heading: hallucination.

In the "Three Cantos" of 1917, which appeared in *Poetry*, we can again see evidence of Pound's attempts to dissociate the visionary from the hallucinatory. There, the hallucinatory experience is called *phantastikon*.

> And shall I claim;
> Confuse my own phantastikon,
> Or say the filmy shell that circumscribes me
> Contains the actual sun;
> confuse the thing I see
> With actual gods behind me?
> Are they gods behind me?
> How many worlds we have![34]

Hugh Kenner uses this passage to suggest that Pound, in *The Cantos*, includes such material ("unreality") only to confront it with the "reality" of facts. Kenner writes,

> in Canto III, sitting on the customhouse steps and gazing across the Grand Canal at splendors he has not the money to visit, he imagines gods floating in the azure air, and indulges (Cantos IV–VII) a kaleidoscope of fancies, visions, glimpses, flickering wonders that merge into postwar unreality. It is like a compendium of Pound's early poetry, economically rewritten: then suddenly cut off and confronted with an order of reality which that early poetry always felt it ought to transcend: authentic documents that survive from the past.[35]

Insofar as this is a characterization of Pound's use of actual historical documents in his poetry it is undeniably true, but it is a mistake—and a symptomatic one—to set documentary fact *against all* extraordinary experience, as Kenner's "kaleidoscope of fancies, visions, glimpses" does, for this is to conflate what were for Pound two discrete kinds of experience.

We have the other, visionary kind of experience in the same 1917 canto, and it is given by Pound as a rebuke of the "phantastics" of Browning as well. Here is his direct address to Browning:

> And set out your matter
> As I do, in straight simple phrases:
> Gods float in the azure air,
> Bright gods, and Tuscan, back before dew was shed,
> It is a world like Puvis'?
> Never so pale, my friend,
> 'Tis the first light—not half light—Panisks
> And oak-girls and the Maenads
> Have all the wood. Our olive Sirmio
> Lies in its burnished mirror,
> and the Mounts Balde and Riva
> Are alive with song, and all the leaves
> are full of voices.
> "Non è fuggito."
> "It is not gone." Metastasio
> Is right—we have that world about us.[36]

For Pound there is no quarrel between visions and facts, because visions are facts; it is hallucinations that are unreal. This distinction is true for *The Cantos* as a whole, though nowhere as explicit as we find it in "The New Therapy."

Pound realizes that if his glandular speculations argue for our understanding the two kinds of phenomena as discrete, we cannot "introspect" glandular action, and experientially there must be another way of distinguishing between the two kinds of experiences that the age has lumped. For Pound, the cutting edge seems to be "orderliness." In "The New Therapy" he states, "I want to distinguish between the orderly visualization which I presume to be pineal, but which neither confuses nor annoys the visionary, and D.T.'s, or any other sort of hallucination."[37] If we don't follow Pound in his dissociation, it seems that he is deeply ambivalent about "extraordinary" experience, but if we do, it becomes apparent that he is drawn to what he calls visionary experiences but abhors experiences he deems to be hallucinatory. If he distrusts experiences that disorganize the mental faculty, if he derides the lotophagoi and what he calls the "taozers," he is nonetheless drawn to the visionary side of the troubadours, to Richard of St. Victor, to Dante and Iamblichus, and many other mystics.

Significantly, Pound's dissociation of pineal, visionary experience from pituitary, hallucinatory experience, is not to be found in Berman's exposition of glandular effects. Here, as in the relation of Pound's "Postscript" to Gourmont's *Physique*, we find that the Poundian recital is highly colored by inferences drawn from his own life. Berman thinks all imagination, both ordered and diseased, derives from pituitary influence, not only, as Pound suggests, hallucinatory psychic events. According to Berman,

> *Psychologists distinguish between the constructive imagination that expresses itself in an ordered activity and the unbalanced fancies of the fearful neurotic for example. The post-pituitary confers the lability of the underlying state of brain in all of these imaginative tincturings of conciousness. The constructive imagination, one of the few truly precious gifts of personality, is probably the expression of a certain balanced activity of the ante-pituitary and the post-pituitary.*[38]

In reading Berman I often wondered why Pound chose to fasten his visionary experiences on the pineal gland at all. There were a good many reasons not to, in that Berman singles out the pituitary, slighted by Pound in reverse proportion to his embroidering the pineal, for all manner of praise. And why does Pound ignore the description of thyroid-dominant constitutions, the language of which recalls Pound's own prose?

> *Sensitivity, the ability to discriminate between grades of sensation or acuteness of perception is another thyroid quality. Just as the thyroid plus is more energetic, so is he more sensitive. He feels things more, he feels pain more readily, because he arrives more quickly at the stage when the stimulus damages his nerve appara-*

tus. The electrical conductivity of his skin is greater, sometimes a hundred times greater, than the average.[39]

Why does Pound dispute Berman's claim that the pineal retrogresses after adolescence and Berman's only characterization of a mature personality in which the pineal has failed to atrophy as a "chubby debonair irresponsible"?[40]

The answer turns, I think, on a very few suggestive phrases in Berman's book relating to the pineal. As Pound noted in his recital, included in the composition of the pineal is a pigment similar to that found in the retina of the eye. Berman also argues that the pineal might influence the body "by varying the degree of light ray reaction,"[41] in other words, that it might influence our receptivity to light. For Berman this corroborates the theory that the pineal is "the ghost of a once important third eye,"[42] but as we have seen Pound rejects this interpretation. He seems to think instead that the retinal pigment in the pineal is not only related to our receptivity of external light, but of "inner light." That Pound could build up his "pineal speculations" on such slight evidence, indeed in the face of the evidence, argues how important it was to him to arrive at a synthesis of the visionary and the physiological.

It is also quite possible that Pound, in his eccentric reading of Berman, was not only appealing to his experience. It is perhaps even likely that he fastened on the pineal gland in particular because of the place it holds in theosophical tracts on the body—which he could easily have known from Yeats or the Quest Society or elsewhere. In any case, Pound's account and the theosophical account do correspond on a number of points. In Pound's recital, the pineal gland holds a medial position in the perception of outer light and inner light, while "in occultism the pineal gland is regarded as a link between the objective and subjective states of consciousness; or, in exoteric terminology, the visible and invisible worlds of Nature."[43] Furthermore, in the occult account the pineal gland is related to the aura that surrounds the head, which in turn is described in terms which recall Pound's "light around the body":

Seen clairvoyantly, the pineal gland is located near the center of a magnetic field or aura varying from twelve to sixteen inches in di-

*ameter. This aura has no exact or definite boundaries, nor are its
radiations entirely uniform. Rather, it appears as a pulsing, flickering field of energy which becomes intensified under stimulation or
irritation, and fades to an almost imperceptible condition as the
result of extreme mental or vital exhaustion.*[44]

Pound had his own ideas about how it ought to be stimulated!
The crystals which he thought might be implicated in "the sensation of light" (inner light), here are seen as the source of the aura
surrounding the head: "Further examination shows that in the
small granules is the source of the star-like light; they glow, not
with an inherent energy, but as though fluorescent."[45] The corre-
spondences are not exact, nor can we be sure that Pound was familiar with the glandular aspect of theosophical thought, but
Pound's radical reading of Berman must have some basis, and although his own experience of extraordinary states may well explain
his interest in the subject, the peculiar slant of the reading must
have some other source. We can infer from the nature of Pound's
speculations that his source was probably an occult text, theosophical or otherwise.

It is, perhaps, characteristic of Pound's modus operandi that
he should be explicit about visionary experience, a subject on
which he is usually cryptic, in an essay ostensibly devoted to physiology. Be that as it may, "The New Therapy" goes a long way toward helping us grasp the experiential basis of Pound's vocabulary
of light, which is clearly for Pound the vocabulary of vision. Pound,
in describing pineal, visionary experience, speaks of "light, or the
sensation of light," and the "sense of vision, sense of light flowing
along the nerves and making one aware where one's hands are in
the dark. luminosity in vision, 'gates of beryl and chrysoprase effect.' " In "light, or the sensation of light," I think we can safely
see not only a reference to experience, but to the "light not of the
sun" of *The Cantos.* The "gates of beryl and chrysoprase effect"
returns us to the "bulwarks of beryl and chrysoprase" of "The
Flame," where we have already demonstrated a sexual context and
argued for the presence of vision (an argument which here receives independent confirmation). Both these "light effects," the

one turning inward and the other outward, are themselves linked to the experientially verifiable "sense of light flowing along the nerves and making one aware where one's hands are in the dark." We must see this, I think, as a weak experience of what can reach visionary intensity in certain kinds of erotic encounters, remembering the link to Gourmont's *Physique*, which Pound insists upon in "The New Therapy," and the glandular, if not gonadal, bearing of Berman's thesis on sexuality. If this feeling of light flowing along the nerves is only a weak manifestation of what Pound knew at a greater intensity, it is, nonetheless, one of the best aids we have for feeling our way toward an understanding of what Pound meant by "the body of light."

It should be apparent that the experiences which Pound designates "pineal" in "The New Therapy" were not new to him in 1922. Rather, Pound has tried to provide a physiological basis for experiences which had preoccupied him for years and which have a large place in his poetry, from "Hilda's Book" on. That Pound chose to write about these experiences in his poetry from the experiential, rather than the glandular side, was, poetically, certainly a happy choice. "The New Therapy" is of limited use for explicating particular poems, except to the degree that it prepares us to see visionary experiences figured in them and sensitizes us to Pound's visionary vocabulary.

Both the "Translator's Postscript" and "The New Therapy" testify to Pound's continuing preoccupation with erotic, "unofficial mysticism" and demonstrate that Pound was prepared to pursue his belief that the body is not evil right into the physiological. They provide, as well, corroborating evidence for my reading of "Psychology and Troubadours" as a cryptic text, and they will do the same for the interpretation of Pound's "Cavalcanti" to follow. If Pound's physiology is naive enough to seem at times like fable, there is an implicit point of view which informs all his speculations—that sexuality can be a door to extraordinary experience—and charting the outlines of this informing reveals, as we have seen, a good deal about the nature of Pound's preoccupations. Like all good diversions, it teaches.

"Cavalcanti": That the Body Is Not Evil

*The desire of the candidate, or of the "mystic" if one can still em-
ploy that much abused term, is to get something into his con-
ciousness, as distinct from getting it into the vain locus of verbal
exchanges.* Pound, "Terra Italica"

The "Medievalism" essay, titled "Cavalcanti," is acknowledged as
perhaps the most important essay Pound ever wrote;[1] it is, unfortunately, also one of the most difficult. That there is nothing
ephemeral about Pound's interests in Cavalcanti and the worldview that stands behind him is clear from Pound's dating the essay
1910–31; and I use the plural "interests" advisedly, because within
the compass of the one essay Pound indulged several, many of
which we will not be taking up. The focus in this chapter will be
on what Pound makes of Cavalcanti, rather than on Cavalcanti
himself. The aspects of the essay that are relevant to Pound's preoccupation with the erotic are "closed," just as in "Psychology and
Troubadours"; they are meant for an elect audience and are "safe"
from the crowd in the same way that Cavalcanti's "Donna Mi
Prega" is safe; hence Pound's use of the beginning of the *envoi*
from Cavalcanti's poem for the epigraph to his own essay: "Safe
may'st thou go my canzon whither thee pleaseth / Thou art so fair
attired" (*LE*, 149). The real difficulty of the essay, as distinct from
the superficial difficulty engendered by the crowding of several lan-
guages into the text, is in the connections between the parts, or
the absence of such connections. Readers are left to make the connections or not, according to their understanding. The scholar's
position is somewhat different, in that Pound's other pronounce-
ments may bridge a gap where unaided understanding might falter.

"Cavalcanti," like much of Pound's work, is in the nature of
a recovery, and the mode of recovery is Gourmontian dissociation.
Just as Pound, as we have seen, dissociated out of the modern
"hallucination" both vision and *phantastikon* to reestablish a distinction which had been largely obscured, in this essay he wants to
perform a related dissociation on the erotic, to counter the "loss of
values . . . due usually to lumping and to lack of dissociation.
The disproved is thrown out, and the associated, or contempo-
rarily established, goes *temporarily* with it" (*LE*, 153, my emphasis). What Pound is trying to get back to is the "new thing in medieval work."

*The Greek aesthetic would seem to consist wholly in plastic, or in
plastic moving toward coitus, and limited by incest, which is the
sole Greek taboo. This new thing in medieval work that concerns
us has nothing to do with Christianity, which people both praise
and blame for utterly irrelevant and unhistorical reasons. Erotic
sentimentality we can find in Greek and Roman poets, and one
may observe that the main trend of Provençal and Tuscan poets is
not toward erotic sentimentality.* [*LE*, 150]

The first danger is to allow "aesthetics" too much weight, especially to the degree that "aesthetics" suggests the aesthete or *l'art
pour l'art*. The second danger is to ignore, or to take metaphori-
cally, the punctuation of this passage, and indeed the whole essay,
with words like "coitus" and "erotic." Proceeding by negation:
Pound insists on what the "new thing" *is not*—it's not erotic sentimentality—but at the same time he is suggesting that it is erotic,
without specifying in what way it is erotic. This is the same strat-
egy we observed in the opening lines of "The Flame":

'Tis not a game that plays at mates and mating,
Provençe knew;
'Tis not a game of barter, lands and houses,
Provençe knew. [*P*, 50]

The erotic is indicated without being specified.
That the "new thing," this "exotic," is *not* sentimental is a
beginning, but the nonsentimental is only one dimension of the

"new thing," and is inadequate as definition. There are other dimensions. One, which Pound first approaches at a high level of
generality, is the matter of the status of the body. Again, Pound
proceeds by negatives: "They [Cavalcanti et al.] are opposed to a
form of stupidity not limited to Europe, that is, idiotic asceticism
and a belief that the body is evil" (*LE*, 150). Within the specifically sexual context this translates as, "Their freedom is not an attack on Christian prudery, because prudery is not a peculiarly
Christian excrescence. There is plenty of prudery in Virgil, and
also in Ovid, where rumour would less lead one to expect it" (*LE*,
151). To be plain, the troubadours and Cavalcanti, on Pound's account, are attacking prudery per se. But this is not to say that they
are affirming license, or libertarian indulgence.

What is the difference between Provence and Hellas? There is, let
us grant, a line in Propertius about ingenium nobis fecit. *But the*
subject is not greatly developed. I mean that Propertius remains
mostly inside the classic world and the classic aesthetic, plastic to
coitus. Plastic plus immediate satisfaction.

   The whole break of Provence with this world, and indeed the
central theme of the troubadours, is the dogma that there is some
proportion between the fine thing held in the mind, and the in-
ferior thing ready for immediate consumption. [LE, 151][2]

This suggests that "not prudery" does not yield license, for it is the
"classical" rather than the Provençal-Tuscan which has incest as
its "sole taboo."[3]

   "Plastic plus immediate satifaction," "plastic to coitus," "plastic moving toward coitus," these are difficult, compact statements
which Pound uses to describe "Hellas." We can isolate in them
two separable, yet related elements. The first is exclusively erotic,
and brings us back to the "matter of delay" as we found it in "Psychology and Troubadours": "the attitude of the Latin *doctor*
amoris [Ovid] and that of the *gran maestro de amor* [Arnaut] are
notably different, as for instance on such a matter as delay. Ovid
takes no account of the psychic function" (*SR*, 97). Pound's
physiological divagations, it will be remembered, revealed the same
dissociation on the physiological level. All of which supports the

criticism of the "classical" we find in the "Cavalcanti." The "new thing" is neither prudery nor "unprudery," but derives from an eroticism of dalliance, an eroticism aimed not at the "immediate satisfaction" of a physical impulse, but at the stimulation of the psyche to visionary perception.

The second element has the erotic as a source, but is formulated in terms of aesthetics. It is the "plastic." Plastic, as applied to the classical, will be seen to be "non-animate" plastic, and the plastic itself the simple accident of embodiment. Commenting on Cavalcanti and those like him (Pound among them):

The Tuscan demands harmony in something more than the plastic. He declines to limit his aesthetic to the impact of light on the eye. . . . Man shares plastic with the statue, sound does not require a human being to produce it. The bird, the phonograph, sing. Sound can be exteriorized as completely as plastic. There is the residue of perception [for the Tuscan], perception of something which requires a human being to produce it. Which even may require a certain individual to produce it. This really complicates the aesthetic. You deal with an interactive force: the virtu in short. [LE, 151–52]

Still proceeding by negations: The "new thing" is not the "Greek perception of visual non-animate plastic." This, also, can be broken down into components: the thing perceived and the mode of perception. With respect to the former, Pound admits that the Greeks do not provide the limiting negative case, which is found in more modern painting.

Certainly the metamorphosis into carnal tissue becomes frequent and general somewhere about 1527. The people are corpus, corpuscular, but not in the strict sense 'animate', it is no longer the body of air clothed in the body of fire; it no longer radiates, light no longer moves from the eye, there is a great deal of meat, shock absorbing, perhaps—at any rate absorbent. It has not even Greek marmoreal plastic to restrain it. The dinner scene is more frequently introduced, we have the characters in definite act of absorption; later they will be but stuffing for expensive upholsteries. [LE, 153]

Not "meat," and then the first affirmation: "the body of air clothed
in the body of fire" (*not* erotic sentimentality). The body perceived and figured by the Tuscans and Pound is wholly "non-
plastic," and the figure is " 'accidental' in the philosophic technical sense. The shape occurs" (*LE*, 152).

Of course, if the thing perceived is wholly "non-plastic" the
mode of perception becomes problematical. The first distinction
here—following Pound's lead—must be a negation: this is not
"sight" as we normally understand it, which is the "impact of light
on the eye" (my emphasis). This is the perception of the body as
plastic; Pound derides even sophisticated works springing from this
kind of perception, such as impressionism. His interest, instead, is
in "interactive" perceptions, in which light again "moves *from* the
eye" (my emphasis) to interact with the light coming to meet the
eye. In Pound's recital of the function of glands, the light proceeding from the eye is called the "pineal" light, or sensation of light,
the "sense of vision, sense of light flowing along the nerves and
making one aware where one's hands are in the dark. luminosity
in vision, 'gates of beryl and chrysoprase' effect."[4] In "The New
Therapy" Pound was trying to establish a physiological basis for a
kind of visionary experience; here that same experience serves as a
standard against which works of art are judged, particularly Tuscan
poetry.

But what is this "interactive" mode of perception that renders
bodies into "the body of air clothed in the body of fire," and the
"objects" of vision radiant: "omnia, quae sunt, lumina sunt"? We
must start with its source in sensuous reality. The reason Pound
chose the "Cavalcanti" essay rather than another place to ridicule
those who believe the body is evil, to assert that the body is not
evil, is that the "residue of perception, perception of something
which requires a human being to produce it," presupposes that the
body is good, for to think the body is evil is to deny the possibility
of the kind of perception Pound is talking about. The body, for
Pound, is intelligent,

*And dealing with it [the interactive force] is not anti-life. It is not
maiming, it is not curtailment. The senses at first seem to project
for a few yards beyond the body. Effect of a decent climate where*

a man leaves his nerve-set open, or allows it to tune in to its am-bience, rather than struggling, as a northern race has to for self-preservation, to guard the body from assaults of weather.

He declines, after a time, to limit reception to his solar plexus. The whole thing has nothing to do with taboos and bigotries. It is more than the simple athleticism of the mens sana in corpore sano. *The conception of the body as perfect instrument of the increasing intelligence pervades. The lack of this concept invalidates the whole of monastic thought. Dogmatic asceticism is obviously not essential to the perceptions of Guido's ballate.* [LE, 152]

The first condition is a decent climate, a climate which encourages sensitivity. Pound is serious about this, and returns to the subject in many places (and it perhaps explains why Eleanor of Aquitaine should have "spoiled in a British climate" [7/24]). Besides his own observations, he may have been thinking of Allen Upward, who argued in *The Divine Mystery* (which Pound reviewed enthusiastically [SP, 403–6]) that "there seem to be definite limits of temperature favourable to human activity, and this philanthropic zone has advanced within historical memory from the latitude of Thebes and Benares to that of London and Berlin."[5] Even in an essay like "Patria Mia" Pound, in characterizing Americans, felt it important to note:

The Englishman, in dealing with the American, forgets, I think, that he has to do with a southerner, a man of the Midi. He thinks, erroneously, that the United States, once a set of his colonies, is by race Anglo-Saxon. New York is on the same parallel with Florence, Philadelphia is farther south than Rome . . . the climate takes up its lordship and decrees the nature of the people resulting. [SP, 102–3][6]

But climate is important only because it encourages feeling, encourages a man to "tune in," leave "his nerve-set open," until the senses seem to extend beyond the extremities of the body: "non razionale ma che si sente," as Pound translates the phrase from "Donna Mi Prega," "not by reason, but 'tis felt" (LE, 159 and 156). Our reason, guided by our materialistic conceptions of what constitutes body (what Pound calls "Rubens' meat"), accepts with difficulty that the senses "at first seem to project a few yards beyond the body," but Pound thinks Cavalcanti's phrase is directed against just this kind of "idea" which keeps us from our own perceptions: "it is against the tyranny of the syllogism, blinding and obscurantist" (*LE*, 159).[7]

Of course, the body *doesn't* feel like meat, no matter what we think of it, though our thoughts certainly color our perceptions; and few of us would have difficulty identifying the kind of perception Pound describes as "pineal" either—"sense of light flowing along the nerves and making one aware where one's hands are in the dark."[8] But Pound is talking about "extraordinary" sensitivity, which we cannot verify with a few moments of *natural demonstration.* Empathy, in this region, is restricted to "elect recipients" (*LE*, 159). The perception of this "something . . . even may require a *certain* individual to produce it" (*LE*, 151, my emphasis). Constitutionally, that individual must be what Allen Upward called a "genius" or a "sensitive." In Upward's words,

Genius is the power of being sensitive to what is divine. The man of genius, the last delicate bud that sprouts from the tree of man, may be compared to the slender wire that rises from the receiving station to catch the unseen message that comes across the sea from an unseen continent. His duty, like the duty of the wire, is to record that message as he receives it.

All other duties are insignificant beside that. I claim for him the right to discharge it. I deny to Humanity the right to put this conductor to the uses of a bayonet or a barrel-hoop, to bend and break it, to do anything with it that unfits it to transmit the messages from Heaven.[9]

Pound was Upward's good student in all of this, the elect and sensitive genius, the language of electricity and antennae, the sense of duty (*SR*, 87, 93)—and after Gaudier-Brzeska died in the trenches of France, the rage against "Humanity": "Quick eyes gone under earth's lid" (*P*, 191).

But not even a genius of sensitivity arrives at such "perceptions" (here merging into visions) at once. The body, being intelligent, is educable; it is a "perfect instrument of the *increasing intelligence*" (my emphasis), and the "sensitive" "declines, *after a time*, to limit reception to his solar plexus" (my emphasis). But that these perceptions should start from the solar plexus is revealing, in that we do not "normally" think of the solar plexus as the most sensitive part of the body. Clearly, in the context, with its coy but persistent erotic cast, Pound means for us—or at least the elect among us—to understand by solar plexus the genitals. The heightened sensitivity of the genitalia in the erotic encounter (remembering the factor of delay) is, as Pound said in "Psychology and Troubadours," the educative aspect of sex. The education is in the perception of the body as "the body of air clothed in the body of fire," and "after a time," in "omnia, quae sunt, lumina sunt," then in the "invisible." A review of the Upwardian "physics" of all this is in order. Pound, in "Psychology and Troubadours," said,

> *our handiest illustrations are drawn from physics: 1st, the common electric machine, the glass disc and rotary brushes; 2nd, the wireless telegraph receiver. In the first we generate a current, or if you like, split up a static condition of things and produce a tension. This is focussed on two brass knobs or "poles." These are first in contact, and after the current is generated we can gradually widen the distance between them, and a spark will leap across it, the wider the stronger, until with the ordinary sized laboratory appliance it will leap over or around a large obstacle or pierce a heavy book cover. In the telegraph we have a charged surface—* produced in a cognate manner—*attracting to it, or registering movements in the invisible aether.*
>
> *Substituting in these equations a more complex mechanism and a possibly subtler form of energy is, or should be, simple enough. . . . the charged surface is produced between the predominant natural poles of two human mechanisms.* [SR, 93–94, *my emphasis*][10]

That we are to substitute the genitals for the "poles" in this equation is by now obvious. This passage also makes it clear that the beloved, as a charged pole, is ultimately dispensable, after she has trained, or perhaps charged, the "human mechanism." The medium has brought the lover into "contact" with the "radiant world."[11]

By Pound's account, the mode of perception in contacts with this visionary reality is "interactive"; are we to understand by this the "interaction" of the man and the woman in the charged encounter, or is the mode of perception interactive vis-à-vis the radiant world as well? Upward, again, provides the best gloss. In *The New Word* he struggled to refocus modern man's perception on the patterned energy he believed to be the experiential reality behind ossified religious traditions.[12] The body, for Upward as for Pound, was intelligent: "Suppose we say, in words we hardly understand, that what we call the Body is a network woven between the tiny Strength Within and the great Strength Without."[13] The interpenetrative relation between the two realms is described by the figure of the "whirl-swirl," in Upward's words, "a line turning from a round into an end and back into a round. The line going inward is the whirl, and the line coming outward is the swirl. It goes in black and comes out white."[14] But this is just a figure, almost a mathematical figure at that. In the realm of matter, the interpenetrative nature of the relation of the two realms is clearer. Here, Upward takes as his figure the waterspout:

In the ideal waterspout, not only does the water swirl upward through the cloud-whirl, but the cloud swirls downward through the sea-whirl. To make their passage through each other easier for the trained mind to follow, let us change the water into air, and the cloud into ether.

   The ideal waterspout is not yet complete. The upper half must unfold like a fan, only it unfolds all around like a flower-cup; and it does not leave the cup empty, so that this flower is like a chrysanthemum. At the same time the lower half has unfolded in the same way, till there are two chrysanthemums, back to back. In one the air is whirling inward, and the ether swirling outward; in the other it is the ether that whirls, and the air that swirls.

   Now let us change the air into ether, and the ether into

ethereon, and so on into more "perfect fluids," till we have pure strength whirling in on all sides and swirling out again.[15]

With respect to our relation to the world about us, this translates as follows (the world within being the "swirl"):

the creation we behold is not the complete record of the whirl. Of course I do not confine the meaning of the word behold to sight. But it is vulgarly confined to those ways of strength which are detected by the outward organs known as the five senses, or, more carefully speaking, to those ways whose impressions are recorded by the body distinctly enough for us to read.[16]

It is just these "vulgar confines" which Pound seeks to exceed; he means to extend the range of our "interactive" perceptions, to "register" ever more subtle movements "in the invisible aether."[17]

The very dryness of this account approaches the then modern conceptions of energy, which Pound characterized as "unbounded undistinguished abstraction."[18]

For the modern scientist energy has no borders, it is a shapeless 'mass' of force; even his capacity to differentiate it to a degree never dreamed by the ancients has not led him to think of its shape or even its loci. The rose that his magnet makes in the iron filings, does not lead him to think of the force in botanic terms, or wish to visualize that force as floral and extant (ex stare). [LE, 154]

Presumably, for Pound, the mode of perception of the modern scientist is not interactive, but reactive. This would have led to the development of syllogisms about the nature of energy, which in turn blind the modern to the experience of "patterned energy." The rose in the iron filings, and other "signatures" in nature, are manifestations in matter of this "patterned energy" which can be observed through ordinary sensuous modes of perception, but they are manifestations of an energy which may be experienced directly by the sensitive through the extraordinary modes of perception described here.[19]

The basis in experience:

We appear to have lost the radiant world where one thought cuts through another with clean edge, a world of moving energies 'mezzo oscuro rade' [from the text of "Donna Mi Prega," where it reads "mezzo schuro luce rade," which Pound translates as "In midst of darkness light light giveth forth"], 'risplende in sè perpetuale effecto' [from "Donna Mi Prega" again, translated "it ever is unstill, Spreading its rays"], magnetisms that take form, that are seen, or that border the visible, the matter of Dante's paradiso, the glass under water, the form that seems a form seen in a mirror, these realities perceptible to the sense, interacting, 'a lui si tiri' ["Donna" a third time, said of love, that he "draweth all to him" ("a llui si tirj")], untouched by the two maladies, the Hebrew disease, the Hindoo disease, fanaticisms and excess that produce Savonarola, asceticisms that produce fakirs, St Clement of Alexandria, with his prohibition of bathing by women. [LE, 154]

This passage is the clearest prose exposition of the "interactive" experience of a genius of sensitivity Pound ever published. This is the world which Pound maintained is available through an erotic medium to the "sensitive," and they are "realities perceptible to the sense." The examples are still *figurative*, not the thing itself, but, as he said of the "Donna Mi Prega," "the phrases correspond to definite sensations undergone" (*LE*, 162).

The individual elements of the passage, as a rare positive statement of Pound's beliefs about the radiant world, ask glossing. It is worth the minute it requires to take a glass from the cupboard and hold it under water in full sunshine (a swimming pool will do, though perhaps a lake for more poetic natures). The light catches in the glass, but at the same time the glass itself takes on a liquidity, and the result is a brilliant form distinct yet not separate from the surrounding medium. This figures an experience of the "radiant world"; "magnetisms that take form" (the rose in the steel dust) both manifest a formal energy and figure the sensitive's experience, which may be "seen" but may only "border on the visible," be "sensed."[20] The form in the mirror, as I argued earlier, seems to be another medium of approach to the radiant world, and is best understood in light of "On His Own Face in a Glass" of

Personae. There Pound comments on the vagaries of the form seen in a mirror, when the mind is persuaded to set aside the idea of what the image coming back should look like.[21] In the exclamation at the prohibition against women bathing there is another jibe at prudery, but it is significant as well that in the early poem "Canzone: Of Angels" he used bathing women to figure the visionary movement of the beloved in the realm of fluid force. The Italian phrases in the passage, from the "Donna Mi Prega," and the reference to Dante's *Paradiso,* are descriptive of the quality of this radiant, interactive experience, and assertions that their "matter" is experientially linked to what he is here calling the "radiant world." We are left to climb along these figures to the experience that engendered them as best we can.

We are ready now to recur to the aesthetic dimension of Pound's essay on "Cavalcanti," and it will behoove us to do so, since the first two sections of the essay are cast in aesthetic terms. Against "niggled" sculpture and "bulbous excrescence" in architecture, against the "corpuscular" in painting, against Greek "non-animate plastic," "Rubens' meat," and Petrarch, Pound sets works in which "the god is inside": "St. Hilaire its proportions," the "best Egyptian sculpture," "the Quattrocento portrait bust," Botticelli, Ambrogio Praedis, Cavalcanti, Daniel. The distinction is not bound to any particular art; Pound cites examples from architecture, sculpture, painting, and poetry.

"The god" which is inside is the "residue of perception," interactive perception, of the radiant world. The forms seen (with visionary overtones) are rendered in the work of art: "In Guido the 'figure', the strong metamorphic or 'picturesque' expression is there with purpose to convey or to interpret a definite meaning" (*LE,* 154). This, of course, relates to Pound's—and Upward's—insistence on the role of the artist as an interpreter of the divine, not ornamental, not art for art's sake. The genius apprehends the formal energy, then "the force is arrested, but there is never any question about its latency, about the force being the essential, and the rest 'accidental' in the philosophic technical sense. The shape occurs" (*LE,* 152). The "inside" is not, then, a matter of place (difficult to conceive in the case of poetry anyway), but of the arresting of the formal and fluid force in the work of art, where it remains latent, apparent to the eye of "present knowers."

The quality of the perception, of course, coupled with the technical competence which will allow the artist to embody that perception, determines the quality of the work. Pound realizes that the form of a work can be "accidental" (contingent) without that work interpreting the realm of fluid force: "In the case of the statue of the Etruscan Apollo at Villa Giulia (Rome) the 'god is inside,' but the psychology is merely that of an Hallowe'en pumpkin. It is a weak derivation of fear motive, strong in Mexican masks, but here reduced to the simple briskness of small boy amused at startling his grandma" (LE, 152). The theory of aesthetics which stands behind is cognate, but the "quality of the sieve" (or education) is inadequate. Aesthetic theory is not enough, though it is a necessary condition. Pound's interest in Cavalcanti and the others rests on their trying to interpret "fine perceptions," sensuous yet visionary, perceptions stimulated, at least at first, by an erotic encounter. This is the "new thing" in medieval art which Pound is at pains to reveal (and conceal):

Having no hope at all
            that man who is base in heart
Can bear his part of wit
            into the light of it,
And save they know't aright from nature's source
I have no will to prove Love's course. [LE, 155]

Throughout the essay Pound casts Cavalcanti as a kind of dangerous fellow within his milieu, a "natural philosopher" rather than a "moral philosopher." At the outset, in accounting for the vogue of "Donna Mi Prega" in the Middle Ages, he asserts Guido "shows leanings toward not only the proof by reason, but toward proof by experiment," which "may have appeared about as soothing to the Florentine of A.D. 1290 as conversation about Tom Paine, Marx, Lenin and Bucharin would to-day in a Methodist bankers' board meeting in Memphis, Tenn" (LE, 149). The tone is comic, but Pound is serious, as his frequent references to natural demonstration, Roger Bacon et al. suggest. Nor is Guido's science a matter of metaphor, as we find it in the English Metaphysicals: "My suggestion is not that Guido is a mere dilettante poetaster dragging in philosophic terms or caught by a verbal similarity" (*LE*, 161) (here with respect to the relevance of Grosseteste's *De luce*). It is the *mode* of thought of the natural philosopher, of a Roger Bacon, that Pound finds in Cavalcanti, not a superficial usurpation of their language.[22]

For proof by experiment to be dangerous, of course, presupposes a worldview based on "stupid authority." This is just the mentality Pound parodies with the Memphis Methodist bankers, the mentality Pound sets Guido against. Guido "wants no proof that contradicts the '*rationes naturales*', he is not jamming down a dogma unsupported by nature. His truth is not against '*natural dimostramento*' or based on authority. It is truth for elect recipients, not a truth universally spreadable or acceptable" (*LE*, 158–59). The first two sentences read like a literate apology for science, but the third, on that assumption, would be anomalous. Scientific method is here praised for its ability to sweep away syllogisms based on authority—we are expecting "nothing without proof"— but scientific method, as it is commonly understood, requires replicability, and should be on these grounds "universally spreadable" *and* "acceptable," at least theoretically. That Pound should assert the opposite is suggestive.

The explanation, in light of the preceding analysis, is predictable. Remembering that Cavalcanti's "dangerous thinking" involved "proof by experience or (?) experiment" (*LE*, 158) provides a clue, because though the experimenter who performs an experiment should be more or less interchangeable with any other (he is only a technician), in experience the subject is crucial ("may even require a certain individual to produce it"). Bluntly, the scientific mode can only be applied in a case like this by those who have the experience in question: "elect recipients." We are, indeed, back to the distinction we made in commenting on Pound's "Translator's Postscript" to *The Natural Philosophy of Love*; *natural demonstration* is being brought to bear on the sensitive's experience of himself, the beloved, and the world around him, not as things but as interactions in the realm of fluid force. This is a science of sensation, science applied to "definite sensations undergone." And the comparison to Pound's (bizarre) theorizing in the "Postscript" is not as wild as it might appear; Pound himself says of Cavalcanti that "at times and with some texts before me, 'natural dimostramento', would seem to imply almost biological proof" (*LE*, 178).

Pound's enthusiasm for the scientific method, of course, is not limited to its application to sensation, though that *is* his particular interest when it comes to the "certain emotional colours" available to the sensitive in an erotic encounter. His belief in the importance of exact perception is almost religious in its fervor; he translated Richard of St. Victor's "Amare videre est," as "To love is to perceive" (*SP*, 71) for good reason. It is on this basis that the naturalist Agassiz takes his place among the heros of *The Cantos*. Exact perception dissolves dogma and reveals "signatures" in nature, visible "accidents" of invisible forces.

A good deal of the difficulty of Pound's "Cavalcanti" derives from a submerged tendentiousness on Pound's part, and not only in the ostensibly explanatory sections ("Partial Explanation"). For instance, a section entitled "The Vocabulary" is as much a sustained attack on Luigi Valli's *Il Linguaggio Segreto di Dante e dei "Fideli d'Amore"*[23] as it is an essay on the "terminologie Cavalcantis." Pound praises the volume as a useful "irritant" but insists that it is inapplicable to the "Donna Mi Prega." What Pound does not find is support for Valli's "theories *re* secret conspiracies, mystic brotherhoods, widely distributed (and uniform) cipher in 'all' or some poems of the period" (*LE*, 173). Pound's reaction seems excessive; if Valli's theories provided a useful irritant they must have been nonetheless *very* irritating for Pound to have scrawled so much against them: not only in "Cavalcanti" but in "Terra Italica," and *Guide to Kulchur*.[24] We can safely infer, I think, that Pound's choler is based on the realization that to accept Valli's "code cipher" reading is to reduce Pound's own theories on Cavalcanti to ashes. If the *donna* in "Donna Mi Prega" is as Valli suggests "un adepto"—a "fellow lodge member" in Pound's redaction—then there is no "natural demonstration" and no "unofficial" mysticism, because the "elect recipients" would no longer be the constitutionally "sensitive" but card-carrying "iniziati," members of a secret society.

Pound's stance, vis-à-vis Valli, is delicate, in that while he wants to discredit Valli's position he wants as well to maintain *a* "mystical" element, and the arguments coming to Pound are polarized around literal, simply sexual readings and allegorizing readings à la Valli. We get, therefore, odd statements like "Valli must try to imagine *what sort of mysticism* his adepts and neophytes practised, and what its effect would have been, for certainly neither Frederick II nor Cavalcanti were openly famed as ascetics" (*LE*, 181, my emphasis), and "If he [Valli] will throw out his suppositions, and his inept evidence and stick to the unsolved enigmas one can give him many passages on which the, by him, hated positivisti could gain no foothold whatever" (*LE*, 180). Pound is with Valli insofar as he sees some kind of "mysticism" in the poem which "positivisti" are always going to doubt, but only that far. For Pound the lady must be real to serve as a medium for the lover, and predictably he punctuates his essay with assertions to that effect, contra Valli. So we find that "perhaps Guido was enamoured as Dante has remarked of a certain Madonna Primavera, who, as Dante does not remark, had set the dance in Langue d'Oc and in Lemosi" (*LE*, 180) (and here we must read, I think, all of "Psychology and Troubadours," as Madonna Primavera provides an "apostolical link" between Provence and Tuscany). And we find him quoting an early exegesis of the canzone by one Del Garbo, glossing the word *donna*: "Del Garbo is not looking for or admitting any cryptogram, he is concerned with its being a woman old enough to possess knowledge, and of good family. The question of noble blood, etc., was then . . . a subject of interest and debate" (*LE*, 182). These are topics, we are to understand, which would not come up in the case of "un adepto." And again, glossing the phrase "Discerne male," Pound comments, "The interpreter with too great a thirst for metaphysics, and metaphysical interpretations [Valli et al.], must not rush over this phrase. It blocks several too abstract, too deadly intellectual decodings. If the *Amor* is limited to *amor sapientiae* why drag in this phrase and why also drag in the *che si sente?*" (*LE*, 187).

The direction all this is tending is, I trust, apparent. Just as it is necessary for Pound to deride "idiotic asceticism and a belief that the body is evil" if he is to champion "mediumistic" sexuality, he must parry Valli's suggestions that Cavalcanti is writing in ciphers if he is to keep Cavalcanti as a sensitive practitioner of an erotic and "unofficial" mysticism. Hence his insistence that the *donna* in the "Donna Mi Prega" is a flesh-and-blood lady. The "Cavalcanti" essay as a whole is not, as a cursory reading might suggest, a ragbag. The aesthetics, the literary criticism, the criticism of asceticism, the morals, all take as their standard an exceptional eroticism which Pound nowhere in the essay directly enunciates. For those readers without an inkling that there is such a standard, Pound's procedure must be puzzling. Indeed, the experience of working a jigsaw puzzle provides a good if banal analogue of reading the essay. An individual piece is often inscrutable; it's only when it is placed in the puzzle that we recognize that pink tip as nose. Pound presumes that "present knowers" *know* what the puzzle looks like as a whole, that they will recognize the pieces for what they are.

In the following chapters on *The Cantos* there will be ample opportunity to recur to Pound's "Medievalism" essay, and the language and ideas of the "Donna Mi Prega" itself will be seen to provide important clues to the erotic dimension of the Pound epic. In the foregoing pages I have simply been at pains to demonstrate that Pound's reading of Cavalcanti is thoroughly infused by a covert preoccupation with mediumistic sexuality. The essay is in itself an important document for understanding Pound's psychology, and as the following chapters will demonstrate, it is equally valuable for an understanding of Pound's mature poetry.

Before passing on to *The Cantos* it is worth pausing for a minute over Pound's interest in "medievalism" in its broader outlines. In the explication of "Psychology and Troubadours" and "Cavalcanti" it has become apparent that Pound's interest in me-

dieval poetry was more than a fascination with its metrics and
motz el son. Pound took a substantive interest in "medieval work,"
and whether or not his interpretations of medieval poetry are accurate they are indicative of his own predilections. Visionary sexuality is in Pound's mind one of the great strains of medievalism,
both as a subject and as an instigation. Pound's theories about this
"new thing" in medieval work are not specific with respect to author; indeed, his theory is general.

   In "Terra Italica," apparently written just after "Cavalcanti,"
Pound comments on a series of booklets then appearing in Italy—
a series entitled, though he doesn't mention it, Biblioteca dei
Curiosi. "Terra Italica," like "Psychology and Troubadours" and
"Cavalcanti," is shot through with cryptic allusions to mediumistic
sexuality, but it also reveals how inclusive his theories are (though
again the general reader will find it difficult to follow through on
the clue): "Taken together the brochures 'Sacerdotesse' and
'Misteri di Mithra', will allow the reader to disentangle more confusions [about medieval work] than any commentary on medieval
poetry yet written" (*SP*, 56). *Sacerdotesse e Danzatrici nelle Religioni Antiche*[25] is the more important of the two because *I Misteri
di Mithra* is the negative case—"Mithraic 'evil,' "[26] antiflesh, another component, Pound realizes, of the medieval. *Sacerdotesse*
is not, actually, all that original, as Pound himself admits, "I don't
assert that most of the information conveyed is not to be found
elsewhere in voluminous works (Maspero, Frazer, etc.) or that a
good deal of it could not be dug out of encyclopedias circulated in
England and America in 'sets' " (*SP*, 55). The anonymous author of *Sacerdotesse* provides a focus on what Pound tags "the
light from Eleusis." But whereas Pound's interest is largely in its
subjective dimensions, *Sacerdotesse* is strictly objective and historical—the role of priestesses in "pagan" religions. With respect
to Eleusis—and indeed generally—the booklet is concerned with
hierogamia—ritual coupling: "la sacerdotessa rappresentava per-
sonalmente Demetra e compiva il rite simbolico della jerogamia
(matrimonio sacro) col Jerofante che, a sua volte, rappresentava
Zeus."[27] The booklet goes on to demonstrate the presence of
"prostituzione sacra" in a great many "antiche" cults. The exis-

tence of such practices is a well-known fact. What is telling is that
Pound thought a knowledge of them would "disentangle more
confusions" about *medieval* poetry than "any commentary . . .
yet written." It is, of course, a position which is consistent with
his "reading" of Cavalcanti, as we have discussed it in this chapter,
but the breadth of his theorizing is more apparent, its sexual implications a little more naked.

The Cantos: First Assay

What remains, and remains undeniable to and by the most hard-ened objectivist, is that a great number of men have had certain kinds of emotion and, magari, *of ecstasy. They have left indelible records of ideas born of, or conjoined with, this ecstasy.* Pound, *Guide to Kulchur*

Simple magnitude, not to mention complexity, makes any "first assay" of *The Cantos* a perilous encounter. To circumscribe the subject, in this chapter I will focus on a single canto—25. The choice is not entirely arbitrary; 25 is not an extraordinarily diffi-cult canto among those in which Pound's visionary eroticism plays a large part, and the background material for the canto will prove useful for the fuller treatment of the theme to follow. But more important, the analysis of a connected passage in the context of a single canto has the positive virtue of revealing Pound's poetic strategies and providing a sense of the relation of mediumistic sexuality, as a subject, to some of *The Cantos'* more celebrated themes.

Pound's presentation of the "ideogram" of visionary eroticism in *The Cantos* is not less cryptic than his published comments in prose or early poetry. Nothing in *The Cantos*, it seems, is easy, and the difficulty increases exponentially when Pound is as set on concealing (from the *vulgus*) as he is on revealing (to the elect), as in this case. "Keys" of all sorts, in such a situation, take on an exaggerated attractiveness, perhaps a dangerous attractiveness, in-sofar as a key is by nature reductive. However, no piece of evi-dence is to be spurned, and in a notebook for Canto 25 Pound has

left a few clues which will repay our attention. Pound was in general wary of letting his notes get about; for example, he hesitated
sending his own father prose drafts of his sources for the "Seven
Lakes Canto." As he said, "If I fix up a printable version later I
DON'T want rough draft left about."[1] Yet, the notes for Canto 25
are certainly more revealing than any prose drafts for the "Seven
Lakes Canto." There, following a few jottings about the procession of light from the eye versus simple reception—a distinction we
observed in Pound's "Cavalcanti"—we can reconstruct from
Pound's scrawl:

languid move [ment] of the inner body.
    preceding the meat move [ment]

---

moving from wihot [without] the othr [other]
    arms of siva

---

augeides—the gods—[2]

The first two lines of this note are clearly moving within the compass of the previous discussion of Pound's "Cavalcanti"; there is
an ethereal body of some sort, and a fleshly body. However, here
the two are not simply contrasted, their relation is described—
visually rather than abstractly. The body which is perceived by
simple reception—"Rubens' meat"—and the body which is perceived when the light proceeds from the eye, are here seen simultaneously. The ethereal body seems to billow around the fleshly
body, the movements of the ethereal body anticipating the movements of the other. In the second pair of lines the relation between the two bodies seems to be becoming increasingly tenuous;
the ethereal body moves on its own, without a corresponding
movement in the "gross" body. The "arms of siva," no doubt, is
meant to describe the quality of the movement of the ethereal
body, perhaps like the tail of a Chinese kite in a light breeze.
These lines, too, seem to elaborate what the lover *sees.*
    The fifth line, "augeides—the gods," is conceptual, a naming

("augeides" is a misspelling of *augoeides*).[3] Suggestively, "The Augoeides or Radiant Body" is also the title of an essay published in *The Quest* by G. R. S. Mead in 1910,[4] the journal to which Pound contributed his crucial essay "Psychology and Troubadours" in 1912. And since Pound was also in personal contact with Quest Society members during these years, it is very likely that he saw Mead's essay, or was at least familiar with its contents. But we must beware of imagining that Pound "swallowed whole" the Mead redaction of tradition, remembering that such an assumption proved unwarranted in the earlier discussion of the probable effect that Mead's position on Simon Magus had on Pound's "Psychology and Troubadours." There, Pound welcomed Mead's research, but interpreted the record along radically different lines.

Mead's essay on the *augoeides* is principally a presentation of what he was able to glean from his sources about "the radiant body" and is to a large extent simply an anthology of quotations from Platonists, Neoplatonists, and Gnostics. Several from Pound's pantheon of philosophers appear—such as Proclus and Porphyry—but this is perhaps unavoidable in any discussion of the "Platonici." Much of what Mead has collected does seem to bear on Pound's veiled discussions of "subtle bodies." Etymologically, Mead redacts, "In classical Greek, *augoeidēs* is an adjective meaning 'possessed of a form of *augē*', that is of a form of splendour, brightness, brilliance, radiance; hence brilliant, shining, radiant, ray-like, luciform, glorious, etc."[5] The adjectival form later took on substantive significance, and became "the Augoeides as the Radiant Body, or Glorious Vehicle or Vesture of the Soul."[6] Mead's language is, of course, consistent with Pound's descriptions of the "radiant world," if rather more purple.

Mead characterizes the relation of the "Radiant Body" to the fleshly body as follows: "The Augoeides was . . . thought more usually to be centered, as it were a light spark, in the head—that is, its only point of contact with the physical body was imagined to be in the head—whereas the spiritous body, . . . was thought of as pervading the whole gross body and surrounding it."[7] This must give us pause, for the lines quoted earlier from Pound's notebooks for Canto 25 seem to conform to the description of the "spiritous body" rather than to the radiant body. Pound is perhaps misremembering his terms, but perhaps not, in that the light which proceeds from the eye does not seem to be the same light that surrounds the body. Pound may have two separable "vehicles" in mind. If this is so, the intellectual underpinning for the distinction may be derived from an earlier Mead essay (also published in *The Quest*) devoted to the "Spirit Body." Interestingly enough, there we read that "the spirit-body, or spiritous embodiment, was often called the aery or ethereal body."[8] All of which suspiciously recalls Pound's phrase "the body of air clothed in the body of fire."

There is also, in the notes to Canto 25, a curious diagram[9] which suggests, in an occult way, that the subtle bodies of the lovers are joined in this rite.

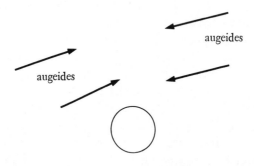

We can safely, I think, see no more here than a shorthand notation of what must be a "visual" experience—the seeing of two subtle bodies joined, either the light which surrounds the body, or the light which proceeds from the eye (the latter seems more likely). It is tempting to see in the arrows the arrows of medieval love poetry, which do proceed from the eye. It is tempting to see, in the circle which marks the joining of the augoeides, a cryptic echo of "the great ball of crystal," particularly given the context. But, again, it seems more profitable to hold to the minimal certainty that the diagram provides a further elaboration of Pound's visionary preoccupations.

Pound, of course, for one reason or another—perhaps in deference to the skeptical among his friends—did not adopt augoeides into the terminology of his ideogram for visionary experience. Indeed, in both his poetry and prose, he chose to avoid terminology that smacked of theosophy. In consequence, the nature of the experiences he was describing has been largely obscured, but he has foiled as well those who would be content with a name, leaving us to clamber back along his descriptions of the psychic events themselves. His eschewal of terms like "augoeides"—except in notes to himself, apparently—reminds us that we haven't captured his thought when we have labeled it (a gnostic and magical belief on our part anyway!). This is the danger presented by Pound's notes for Canto 25; they invite us to end our investigation with a name. The canto itself withholds the name; it "presents":

> And Sulpicia
> green shoot now, and the wood
> white under new cortex
> "as the sculptor sees the form in the air
>   before he sets hand to mallet,
> "and as he sees the in, and the through,
>   the four sides
> "not the one face to the painter
> As ivory uncorrupted:
>   "Pone metum Cerinthe"
> Lay there, the long soft grass,
>   and the flute lay there by her thigh,
> Sulpicia, the fauns, twig-strong,
>   gathered about her;
> The fluid, over the grass
> Zephyrus, passing through her,
>   "deus nec laedit amantes."
> Hic mihi dies sanctus . . . [25/117–18]

Sulpicia in the grass dominates this passage, is present throughout it, provides the persona of the beloved, over which Pound layers, ply over ply, elements of his visionary eroticism. In the first section Pound invokes the "metamorphic moment" by recurring to the motif of man-as-tree—a signature of metamorphosis from

"Hilda's Book" onward. In the *Personae* of 1926 it is most visible in "The Tree," written for Hilda Doolittle when they were both teenagers, but it is also apparent in "A Girl." These two poems deserve to be juxtaposed in this context, and I'll quote them in their entirety. In reading them, we should keep in mind the erotic context suggested by "A Girl," Pound's assertion in "Psychology and Troubadours" that "myths are only intelligible in a vivid and glittering sense *to those people to whom they occur*" (SR, 92, my emphasis), and that in his "Arnold Dolmetsch" Pound described the origin of myth experientially, as a man walking "sheer into 'nonsense'" (LE, 431), giving, suggestively, as an example a man who created a myth to make palatable his experience of having "turned into a tree" (LE, 431). Here is "The Tree":

I stood still and was a tree amid the wood
Knowing the truth of things unseen before,
Of Daphne and the laurel bow
And that god-feasting couple olde
That grew elm-oak amid the wold.
'Twas not until the gods had been
Kindly entreated and been brought within
Unto the hearth of their heart's home
That they might do this wonder thing.
Nathless I have been a tree amid the wood
And many new things understood
That were rank folly to my head before. [CEP, 35]

"A Girl":

The tree has entered my hands,
The sap has ascended my arms,
The tree has grown in my breast—
Downward,
The branches grow out of me, like arms.

Tree you are,
Moss you are,
You are violets with wind above them.

A child—so high—you are,
And all this is folly to the world. [CEP, 186]

In reading these poems we must not deny the "nonsensical" element—a man becoming a tree—by taking cover under the word "metaphor." Pound insists on nonsense with the word "folly" in the last line of each poem. Of course, the objective observer would not see the lover transformed into a tree, but Pound is proceeding by feeling, and he feels that "things do not remain always the same. They become other things by swift and unanalysable process" (*LE*, 431). The erotic encounter (implicit in "The Tree," explicit in "A Girl") occasions the metamorphic moment. That this is true in the passage I have quoted from Canto 25 is an evidential judgment, but the evidence is there, although incomplete. As Hugh Kenner has shown us, the Sapphic fragment had structural implications for Pound, and in his own poetry Pound began to proceed by fragmentation.[10] "The Tree" and "A Girl" are part of the ideogram, even though they are not part of *The Cantos*, and they are evidentially important for our understanding of the Poundian ellipsis in Canto 25; but there are passages in *The Cantos* which bear on this one as well.[11] The most important is in Canto 20, where we read:

The boughs are not more fresh
where the almond shoots
take their March green. [20/89]

For those who haven't perused Pound's notes for Canto 20 this must seem even more elliptical, but this ellipsis is demonstrably explicable, and will help us to bridge the gap in 25. A page later in the published version of 20 we read:

from her breast to thighs.

In the notes these passages are continuous; the comparative "more" is answered by its "than":

The bough is not more fresh
*   where the almond shoots*

take their March green, than she
square from the breasts to thighs.[12]

Thus, the notes to 20 reveal Pound's suppression of the erotic context in favor of the fragment. The evidence suggests a similar procedure in the

green shoot now, and the wood
white under new cortex

of Canto 25.[13]

    If the statement in the "tree motif" which introduces our passage in 25 is, by Pound's definition, mythic, what follows is not. The mode of statement changes, but the subject—Pound's erotic, "unofficial mysticism"—remains the same. That Pound should take up the subject in a different manner immediately following the introduction of the tree motif provides further oblique support for my interpretation of that motif's significance in Canto 25 by the implied cohesion of the text. What Pound does is poach a little from his own prose (*Gaudier-Brzeska*) in describing the ground of the "real" sculptor's work—"the form in the air." In this case, the passage from 25 elaborates what is only a dim hint in the prose: "The real sculptor 'sees' or is aware of, not only all the sides of his work, but of the 'through', that is the diameters that can be passed through it from any angle."[14] Clearly the discussion of Gaudier-Brzeska is couched in technical language, but it is no coincidence, I think, that Pound passes directly from this to Gaudier's "Hieratic Head of Ezra Pound"—which I have already suggested is implicated in Pound's erotic preoccupations. Besides the resonance with his own prose, "as the sculptor sees the form in the air / before he sets hand to mallet" recalls what by Pound's time had almost become a topos, the sculptor seeing his sculpture *in the stone* before he began work. The variation is an interesting one and consistent with Pound's views of the raw materials of art. For Pound, the artist brings his idea, or form, to the material; he does not take his inspiration from it (despite vorticist strictures against models). Beyond that, the "form" which the sculptor sees in the air is described in a way which suggests the subtle bodies Pound's notes lead us to expect in the canto. It's transparent, but visible. It's seen, not imagined. To understand the presence of this "form" in this context, we must recognize that the force of the passage (and the one which immediately follows) is the force of simile: "as the sculptor," "As ivory uncorrupted." The form seen by the sculptor is *like* the form seen by the lover, and it is not like "the one face" seen by the painter, which here conveys simple reception ("Rubens' meat" in the terminology of Pound's "Cavalcanti"). Pound introduces the simile in this context to locate the kind of perception, in visual terms, experienced by the lover. It is a perception of, seemingly, a transparent subtle body. Of course, we can infer the erotic dimension of this passage—that a lover is implicated at all—only by our knowledge of Pound's other works: early poems, prose, and notes. On its own, the difficulty of the passage would be insuperable.

The referent of "As ivory uncorrupted," which follows immediately after the simile of the sculptor's form in the passage under discussion, is problematical. The syntax is too broken to provide many sure clues. The phrase may refer back to the form seen by the lover, but as a visual description it seems unlikely because of the opacity of ivory (though old ivory does have a sheen and sometimes seems to cast light, which would conform to Mead's descriptions of the *augoeides*). But the colon which follows the phrase seems to indicate that the referent is forward, in the passage which follows, with its return to Sulpicia in the grass:

As ivory uncorrupted:
> *"Pone metum Cerinthe"*
Lay there, the long soft grass,
> *and the flute lay there by her thigh,*
Sulpicia . . .

It is Pound who puts Sulpicia in the grass. In volume 3 of the works of Tibullus, where Sulpicia's poems are bound up and where Tibullus addresses poems to her, we do not find her in the grass, with or without a flute. Pound has reworked his material radically, keeping only the love between Sulpicia and Cerinthus (implicit) and the phrase "pone metum Cerinthe, deus nec laedit amantes"

(Put fear aside, Cerinthus. God harms not lovers),[15] and even that phrase is cut into pieces, varied, and shorn of its original context (Sulpicia on her sickbed, comforting Cerinthus). If Pound revised his source so heavily, he must have done it toward some end, and it is that end which we need to discover if we are to comprehend the introductory "As ivory uncorrupted."

By laying Sulpicia in "the long soft grass" Pound effects a localization of the lovers, a localization which is mildly suggestive, undulant, even erotic. The addition of a flute here is suggestive as well. She does not play it; perhaps she has lain it aside, favoring, for the moment, love to song. But beyond the literal level, the flute probably has a phallic significance, not so much as a symbol as a description born from habits of indirection. It's almost a discretion. But in an indiscreet letter to Viola Baxter Jordan, Pound likens the appearance of the phallus to a flute—dissociating "phallus" (erect) from "penis" (flaccid).[16] If we can admit that the flute here is probably (and we can't expect a greater certainty) an oblique description of a phallus,[17] then Pound's distinction between phallus and penis would also be relevant, suggesting not only that she has her lover with her there in the grass but that he is in a state of readiness.

We are, perhaps, getting closer to understanding to what "As ivory uncorrupted" refers. The colon which follows it suggested that the referent was subsequent; there, we found what appears to be a cryptic reference to a phallus. That the "ivory uncorrupted" refers to the phallus is, I think, highly likely. The following passages from other cantos, which are clearly related to 25, provide further evidence for the attribution. From 21:

Phoibos, turris eburnea,
　　　ivory against cobalt,
And the boughs cut on the air,
The leaves cut on the air
The hounds on the green slope by the hill,
　　　water still black in the shadow.
In the crisp air,
　　　the discontinuous gods . . . [21/99]

And from 29:

> Let us consider the osmosis of persons
> nondum orto jubare;
> The tower, ivory, the clear sky
> Ivory rigid in sunlight
> And the pale clear of the heaven
> Phoibos of narrow thighs,
> The cut cool of the air,
> Blossom cut on the wind . . .
>
> .   .   .   .   .   .
>
> The white hounds on the slope . . . [29/145]

These ivory towers are obviously phallic in intent: "rigid in sun-
light." The two passages also exhibit other facets of the ideogram
of visionary eroticism. The "mythic" tree motif is suggested by the
boughs, leaves, and blossoms, here "on the air" or "on the wind."
The apparitional appearance of the gods is suggested by "In the
crisp air, / the discontinuous gods" (*spezzato*). And the hounds
on the green slope recall a passage in Canto 17:

> And the goddess of the fair knees
> Moving there, with the oak-woods behind her,
> The green slope, with the white hounds
>   leaping about her . . . [17/76]

All of which recall the silver hounds of "The Return," who accom-
pany the returning gods:

> Gods of the wingèd shoe!
> With them the silver hounds,
>   sniffing the trace of air! [CEP, 198]

(Gods who, we will later find, "have not returned. They have
never left us' " [113/787].) And all of these poems, with the exception of "The Return," are dawn songs, and from A *Lume
Spento* on Pound wrote an inordinate number of *albas*, aubades,
dawn songs (about this more later). This poetry is thick with associations, but always the thread, never the whole web. It's a poetry that invites turgid critical prose.

If we grant, then, that the ivory of "As ivory uncorrupted" refers to the flute which in turn is phallic, and the whole is descriptive of an erotic encounter, there remains the question of why this ivory should be "uncorrupted." I think it can be understood, in a general way, as an instance of an implicit distinction between two kinds of sexuality in *The Cantos:* clean, hygienic sexuality and unclean, even diseased sexuality (a distinction which crosscuts any question of vision).[18] The "uncorrupted" is an avowal of cleanliness, perhaps even of ritual cleanliness, and is set against the corrupt or polluted sexuality of the defamers—the homosexuality of the Honest Sailor (12/56–57), the "condom full of black-beetles" of the Hell Cantos (14/63), and the "whores for Eleusis" (45/230), to mention only three examples of "corrupted" eroticism.

The passage from Canto 25 under discussion continues:

> *Sulpicia, the fauns, twig-strong,*
>> *gathered about her;*
> *The fluid, over the grass*
> *Zephyrus, passing through her,*
>> *"deus nec laedit amantes."*
> *Hic mihi dies sanctus . . .* [25/118]

The first two lines here return to the mythic mode, the "twig-strong" of the fauns echoing the tree motif, the fauns themselves "mythic" for a state of being. Again, Pound is his own best commentator. In "Religio," Pound wrote:

> *What is a god?*
> *A god is an eternal state of mind.*
> *What is a faun?*
> *A faun is an elemental creature.*
> *What is a nymph?*
> *A nymph is an elemental creature.* [SP, 47]

What Pound means here by "elemental creature," a phrase he would have later avoided, is to be understood in light of the "Note Precedent to 'La Fraisne' " of *A Lume Spento* where Pound quotes one "Janus of Basel":

*"When the soul is exhausted of fire, then doth
the spirit return unto its primal nature and there
is upon it a peace great and of the woodland*

"magna pax et silvestris."
*Then becometh it kin to the faun and the dryad, a
woodland-dweller amid the rocks and streams*
"consociis faunis dryadisque inter saxa sylvarum." [CEP, 8]

And later in the "Note" in his own voice:

*I because in such a mood, feeling myself divided
between myself corporal and a self aetherial "a
dweller by streams and in woodland," eternal because
simple in elements*
"Aeternus quia simplex naturae" [CEP, 8]

The last quotation helps to explain the others, in that not only
does it betray the customary descent to experience, which seems to
stand behind all of Pound's writings on extraordinary events, but
it also identifies the experience as a "mood," and for Pound myths
were explications of "moods." This particular mood, whose statement involves the evocation of fauns, is described in two ways,
which Pound probably understood as two elements or stages of a
single mood. Perhaps "When the soul is exhausted of fire" is the
immediate condition for Pound's "feeling myself divided between
myself corporal and a self aetherial." But most pertinent for our
study, this last state sounds a great deal like the dissociation of the
subtle from the gross body we observed in Pound's notes for Canto
25, when the subtle body moved without a corresponding movement in the corporeal body. The fauns, then, may be a mythic
statement of what the notes describe literally.[19]

From the mythic statement implicit in his treatment of the
fauns, Pound moves back to description in the line that follows,
describing "the fluid" as it passes over the grass. The definite arti-
cle "the" draws our attention to the word "fluid."[20] Here the word
surely indicates what Pound called in "Psychology and Troubadours" "the universe of fluid force" (SR, 92), which the analysis

of that essay suggested was experienced by the lover in moments of visionary perception in the erotic encounter. It touches, as well, on another motif which Pound returns to again and again, which we can here christen "Sub Mare," after the poem of that name, which opens as "The Tree" and "A Girl" close, with a self-conscious recourse to the nonsensical:

It is, and is not, I am sane enough,
Since you have come this place has hovered round me,
This fabrication built of autumn roses,
Then there's a goldish colour, different.

And one gropes in these things as delicate
Algae reach up and out, beneath
Pale slow green surgings of the underwave,
'Mid these things older than the names they have,
These things that are familiars of the god. [CEP, 194]

In our passage, the "Sub Mare" motif is indicated by the fluid's flowing *over* the grass, the very grass Sulpicia is reclining on.

The next line in our passage also appears to be nonsensical: "Zephyrus, passing through her." This may be yet another return to the mythic mode, indeed, the appearance of "Zephyrus" suggests that it is; but Zephyrus here may simply indicate the wind. In light of the evidence adduced to show that Pound was probably writing about the clairvoyant seeing of a subtle body around the gross body of the beloved (Sulpicia), it is possible that this apparently nonsensical passage simply refers to the wind passing through Sulpicia's subtle body, the *augoeides*, rather than through her corporeal body. This reading makes sense of what is otherwise nonsensical, though the skeptical may—understandably—have recourse to some phrase like "rank folly."

There remain, for explication in our passage, only the two Latin phrases. "Deus nec laedit amantes" completes the "Pone metum Cerinthe," as mentioned earlier. I said there that Pound had taken the phrase out of its original context, and it may be that by embedding it in this new context of a visionary erotic encounter, he has refocused its significance; perhaps rather than soothing the fear of the lover at the potential loss of the beloved to death (as in Sulpicia's poem), the phrase is meant as a reassurance for the lover who has "walked sheer into 'nonsense'" (*LE*, 431).

The "Hic mihi dies sanctus" which closes our passage is a particularly interesting one, in that the "mihi" seems to have an autobiographical force, as an authorial intrusion, a temporary setting aside of the mediating personae of Sulpicia and her Cerinthus. Furthermore, the "sanctus," the holiness of the day, confirms the implicit spirituality with which Pound invests the passage throughout. For Pound, Sulpicia and Cerinthus have performed a rite there in the grass. The "sanctus" prescribes the tone of the passage as a whole.

A rereading of the passage, once the spade work has been done on the phrases which constitute it, reveals that it is not as fragmentary as it originally seemed. It is *superficially* fragmented; Pound moves, on the surface of the poem, from one mode of statement to another and back again, suggesting by the merest phrase those other of his poems and prose pieces which we need to recall to make the passage comprehensible (and some works the general reader cannot know, such as his notes). The passage is very elliptical, even excessively elliptical, but beneath the fragmentation there is one experience, approached in many ways. The implied poetics revealed by this passage is not the poetics of Pound the popularizer. There are two *Cantos*, an exoteric *Cantos* and an esoteric *Cantos*, and this passage is from the latter book.[21]

The preceding analysis illuminates what we may call the "poetics of the passage," but Canto 25, as it relates to the erotic medium, has a macrostructure as well. In its larger units 25 is composed of related sets of dichotomies which serve as axes for Pound's thought. Kenner has explicated one of them, the contrast between Titian and Sulpicia as kinds of artists:

we find Titian submitting the low bid for a piece of interior decoration ("the picture of the land battle in the Hall of our Greater Council"), collecting the perquisite, and for 20 years doing nothing.

Here virtu *is entangled in gain. In the middle of Canto XXV, between the minute-books and the documents concerning the disgraceful behavior of Titian, we find a contrasting* virtu, *that of the Roman poetess Sulpicia.*[22]

There is the suggestion of an economic determinism here, of course; the two kinds of seeing we found earlier, the "one face to the painter" and the sculptor's seeing "the four sides" of the "form in the air," are the kinds of seeing granted to Titian (and his ilk) and to Sulpicia (and hers), and the latter—in Pound's universe—comes "not by Usura." But there are also two kinds of sexuality in the canto, the visionary eroticism attributed to Sulpicia, and the simple copulation of the lions caged by the Lord Doge of Venice in a "room timbered (trabesilis) like a cellar":

said lion knew carnally and in nature the Lioness
aforesaid and impregnated in that manner that animals
leap on one another to know and impregnate [25/115]

The relation between these two dichotomies, setting aside the economic question, is simply that the "sculptor's" seeing is generated by an erotic rite; it is a kind of seeing which is not available to those who copulate "in that manner that animals / leap on one another."

The final dichotomy which serves as an axis in the canto is the distinction between the dead gods, gods known by hearsay and ossified in tradition, and the live gods of visionary experience (here perceived by the lovers Sulpicia and Cerinthus, and in the implication of the "mihi" by Pound himself). Pound presents the negative pole through the purgatorial babbling of the damned and a description of the eviscerated state of their gods:

And from the stone pits, the heavy voices,
Heavy sound:
            "Sero, sero . . .
"Nothing we made, we set nothing in order,
"Neither house nor the carving,
"And what we thought had been thought for too long;

"Our opinion not opinion in evil
"But opinion borne for too long.
"We have gathered a sieve full of water."

. . . .

And as after the form, the shadow,
Noble forms, lacking life, that bolge, that valley
the dead words keeping form,
and the cry: Civis Romanus.
The clear air, dark, dark,
The dead concepts, never the solid, the blood rite . . . [25/118]

The positive pole is presented in the description of the appearance
of the live gods, and by a short anthology of paradisical quotations:

And against this [purgatorial existence] the
            flute: pone metum.

. . . .

Form, forms and renewal, gods held in the air,
Forms seen, and then clearness,
Bright void, without image, Napishtim,
Casting his gods back into the νοῦς.

"as the sculptor sees the form in the air . . .
"as glass seen under water,
"King Otreus, my father . . .
and saw the waves taking form as crystal,
notes as facets of air,
and the mind there, before them, moving,
so that notes needed not move. [25/119]

The relation of this axis to the others, in general, can be understood as a question of experience versus hearsay. The lovers renew
their gods through direct experience (remembering the strictures
Pound puts on the meaning of the word "gods"), through an
erotic rite. Those who have no experience, for whom the erotic
connotes mere copulation, are left only with hearsay: "the
shadow, / Noble forms, lacking life." An artist's experience in this
realm, in turn, dictates the nature of his art.

The last passage quoted also provides a clue about just how the gods are renewed in experience, assuming the erotic encounter implicit in the context. It is a clue worth following, because it bears on the larger—visionary—context in which Pound's erotic preoccupations should be understood. We can begin with the word *nous*. In his *Guide to Kulchur* Pound made it quite clear that he did not understand the word as a philosophic abstraction, but as the name of an experience. "The Platonists . . . have caused man after man to be suddenly conscious of the reality of the *nous*, of mind, apart from any man's individual mind, of the sea crystalline and enduring, of the bright as it were molten glass that envelops us, full of light."[23] The language of this passage clearly resonates at the same wavelength as the language in which Pound describes the radiant world available to the lover ("Sub Mare"). Pound, ever the synthetic thinker, without doubt thinks that the reality is in each case the same, though he would have allowed for differences in the approach to that ground. But this is a little broad, in that Canto 25 insists on two kinds of vision—one in which forms are seen (the gods) and one in which no forms are seen (bright void)—and it is the latter which is called *nous*.

In the Pisan Cantos Pound would say of it,

This liquid is certainly a
       property of the mind
nec accidens est   but an element
                         in the mind's make-up
est agens and functions . . . [74/449]

against those who would make it an abstraction or fantasy. Pound seems to have been familiar with this "bright void" as a mental "element" from early on, at least if his "Histrion" (published in *A Quinzaine For This Yule* in 1908) is good witness:

'Tis as in midmost us there glows a sphere
Translucent, molten gold, that is the "I"
And into this some form projects itself:
Christus, or John, or eke the Florentine;
And as the clear space is not if a form's
Imposed thereon,

So cease we from all being for the time,
And these, the Masters of the Soul, live on. [CEP, 71]

Pound doesn't seem as sure of himself in this early production as
he does in *The Cantos*, and there are some significant differences
between the two accounts, but the subject of "Histrion" does appear to be the same as, or at least similar to, the subject of the passage from Canto 25. In both there is a bright void, and the intermittent superposition on that void of forms (gods or "Masters of
the Soul"). The parallel is too strong to be entirely coincidental—
both poems are rooted in experience.

The gods which are cast back into the *nous*, as Pound's notes
to Canto 25 make very clear, are the gods of hearsay, images of the
gods, finally dead gods. The inherited, traditional images are
melted in the experience of the *nous*, like old coins cast back into
a crucible. But they are recast, made new, in the encounter with
the "bright void"; the experience engenders new images of the
gods even as it destroys the old ones.

This "casting" of the gods into the *nous* seems to denote two
concurrent experiences. There is a visual (or visionary) dimension,
a bright void out of which or upon which the gods form, are seen,
intermittently, *spezzato*. But there is also an intellectual dimension. Experience is here shown as a solvent of received ideas. Pound
is always anxious to "make it new," realizing that received ideas
ultimately come between a man and his experience, until a man is
so vested in tradition that he becomes hostile to "natural demonstration." In Canto 25 Pound insists that this process of ossifica-
tion affects good as well as evil ideas:

". . . *what we thought had been thought for too long;*
"*Our opinion not opinion in evil*
"*But opinion borne for too long.* [25/118]

In casting the received gods back into an experience of the *nous*
Pound makes the gods new: "Fac deum!" "Est factus!" (Make a
god! He is made!), as another canto has it (39/195).

There are no surprises in the paradisical anthology of quotations Pound appends to his presentation of the experience pole of
the third dichotomy. There are two more similes, descriptive of the

lovers' experience. The one, discussed earlier, is of the sculptor's seeing the form in the air ("bright gods and Tuscan"), and the other, "as glass seen under water," a phrase from Pound's "Cavalcanti" essay, where it is used to describe the "radiant world." The third phrase in quotation marks, "King Otreus, my father," is an occult reference to Aphrodite, and surely no other goddess would be more appropriate in the context. All three phrases suggest the return into form. Form, then the bright void, then the return into form.[24] Pound has suppressed, in the published version, those connectives which suggest progression, but there is an implicit progress nonetheless. The four lines which follow the reference to Aphrodite also suggest formation:

and saw the waves taking form as crystal,
notes as facets of air,
and the mind there, before them, moving,
so that notes needed not move. [25/119]

That Sulpicia at last plays is an affirmation of the "interpretative function" of art. It "manifests something [that *is* "trobar clus"] which the artist perceives. . . . Constantly he must distinguish between the shades and the degrees of the ineffable" (*SR*, 87). "The gods," Sulpicia's playing, and this passage from Pound's *Cantos* are all in a sense parallel; they are all forms interpretative of the ineffable. Finally, that the notes of Sulpicia's playing should be stable while the mind moves suggests the felt-timelessness of the experience, and recalls the final stanza of "The House of Splendour":

Here am I come perforce my love of her,
Behold mine adoration
Maketh me clear, and there are powers in this
Which, played on by the virtues of her soul,
Break down the four-square walls of standing time. [P, 49]

In the foregoing analysis I have endeavored to demonstrate the complexity and density of portions of Canto 25, to explicate the subtle and multiple allusions, to explain the shifts in the mode of statement; I've shown how the notes and drafts of the canto are in some ways more explicit than the published version, how they suggest the intellectual underpinning and even an intellectual history with a single word like *augoeides*; I have adumbrated the place of the erotic medium in the larger structure of the canto, sketching in three fundamental axes. With the exception of the comments on the structure of the canto, it must be admitted that this analysis *dis*-integrates our feeling for the integrity of the text, in spite of the demonstration that there is a continuity in the subject matter of the passages. This is a disquieting reward for strenuous analysis. One of the lessons suggested by this is that the tonal continuity which holds Canto 25 together for the naive reader, or perhaps we should say the confidence instilled by the felt-certainty of the way it moves, is quite fragile—like the surface tension that keeps water from spilling when we overfill a cup. It also suggests that although there is a continuity in the subject matter, it is a rough continuity—the radiant world, the *nous*, subtle bodies, the gods, myth and descriptions, they all pull toward their own worlds. Each invites us to reduce the text in a particular direction, into a particular vocabulary, but to the extent that we indulge this tendency for any particular phrase we do violence to the other phrases which constitute the passage as a whole. When we indulge it for every phrase, as in this analysis, we are left feeling that the disjunctions are more prominent than the junctions, and the spaces between the lines start to look like canyons.

To push for too tight a fit, to expect the phrases to snap together like puzzle pieces, is to expect too much. All of the phrases, I have tried to suggest, are meant to interpret experience. Experience is always more compact than its representation or the analysis we bring to it. We must trust, I think, that there is an experiential ground here, necessarily imperfectly manifested in the poem that is about it. That Pound has exacerbated the refractoriness of the representation by his kaleidoscopic treatment is certain, and perhaps it is culpable, but what we are left with is a problem of reading. We must give the phrases each their own weight, so that they sound like harmonics of one another, without drowning one another out. If we can recover the sense of felt-continuity, it will no longer be the superficial continuity of tone, but the deeper continuity of experience and understanding.

The Cantos: Second Assay

the light there almost solid
Pound, Canto 95

The bulk of the preceding chapter is a little disquieting, considering how few lines from Canto 25 actually came under analysis.
This bulk suggests that while the analysis of consecutive passages
tells us a great deal about Pound's methods of proceeding, and
about the place of the erotic rite in the larger thematic canvas of
an entire canto, such analysis is impractical as an approach to the
erotic medium in *The Cantos* at large. The fragmentation of the
subject matter makes the explication of even a short passage a
matter of some weight, and there are a great many passages in
The Cantos which bear on our subject. However, most of these
passages are constructed from a fairly small number of "radicals"
of Pound's ideogram for the erotic medium. Again and again these
radicals, or topics, are introduced into the text, sometimes by as
little as a single word ("unstill," from the "Donna Mi Prega"),
sometimes by several connected lines, but never wholly. What we
get is pieces, fragments. To reconstruct whole radicals, or something approximating wholes, it is necessary to refer to early poems,
prose, and the full range of cantos, from "And then went down to
the ship" to the last phrase of Canto 120. Even then, a good many
of the radicals seem to be incomplete, and were perhaps never truly
whole except in the integrity of Pound's experience of his life and
ideas. In this chapter and the next, then, I will present a number
of topics related to Pound's ideas on the erotic medium, in the
belief that this approach will enable the reader to recognize and

evaluate fragments of the subject which might otherwise remain occult, "and therefore tending" toward a fuller understanding of the place of the erotic medium in *The Cantos* as a whole. I will not, however, recapitulate those items I dealt with at length in previous chapters, such as the "tree motif," in the belief that the treatments there were adequate to sensitize the reader to those topics. In this section I will restrict my analysis to the externals of "this rite," wherever possible, leaving the subjective dimension to the next chapter.

Kenner has a chapter in his *Pound Era* entitled "The Sacred Places"—a suggestive phrase. The visionary colors of Pound's eroticism have their places as well, and their climes, as already discussed in previous chapters. Pound seriously believed that climatological influences played a major role as a precondition for the development of a sensibility capable of registering vision. References to latitude are always suspect, and in the prose where they occur more prominently, they deserve close attention. Longitude may also be a factor, though one suspects, for cultural rather than climatological reasons. In his "Religio," Pound cryptically, toward the end, begins to talk about "this rite," without giving much in the way of hints about what the "this" might refer to, though it is likely that he has this erotic rite in mind:

> *What are the gods of this rite?*
> *Apollo, and in some sense Helios, Diana in some of*
> *her phases, also the Cytherian goddess.*
> *To what other gods is it fitting, in harmony or in*
> *adjunction with these rites, to give incense?*
> *To Koré and to Demeter, also to lares and to*
> *oreiads and to certain elemental creatures.* [SP, 48]

These are the factotums of Pound's erotic celebrations, albeit cast in a lighter vein. Pound ends his "Religio" with the longitudinal:

> *Are these things so in the East?*
> *This rite is made for the West.* [SP, 48]

Pound's apprehensions and misapprehensions about the role of ecstasy in the East have been well documented.[1] That Pound's

usual response to eastern forms of spirituality was suspicion (of
charlatanry) or derision (at asceticism) seems beyond doubt. But
H.D., in her *End to Torment,* reports that Pound, in his
teenage years, was for a time enamored enough with the East
to introduce her to a "series of Yogi books."[2] One wonders whether
there were any Tantric books among them, but that's fishing.
Later, while writing Canto 20, Pound toyed with an oriental echo,
or rhyme, for the tradition of mediumistic eroticism he found in
the West. He described a pair of teahouses with signs out front;
one of them read "Copulation and contemplation, or the WIsdom
of the East,"[3] and the other had the same sign, but with the key
words reversed and the second phrase in French. That subject
rhyme did not make it into the final version, perhaps because it
was too explicit, perhaps because Pound wanted to keep his ideal
East more exclusively Confucian, an emblem of right order, or
perhaps because Pound thought that there simply wasn't an equivalent oriental tradition.

But this is only geography on a mass scale; Kenner has specific
places in mind when he writes of Pound's "sacred places," and,
indeed, "this rite" has its temples though they are all in ruins
(Malatesta's Tempio, for Ixotta, rhymes). At Pisa he would re-
affirm them, refuse to surrender them:

temples
        plural. [74/ 434]

The four most important of them are Sirmione, Montségur,
Terracina, and Eleusis.

Sirmione, "the haunt of Catullus," as Pound calls it in Canto
76, is a peninsula, jutting into Lake Garda (Lago di Garda), in
Northern Italy. It's a place with literary associations. Catullus
addressed a poem to it:

Paene insularum, Sirmio, insularumque
ocelle, quascumque in liquentibus stagnis
marique vasto fert uterque Neptunus,
quam te libenter quamque laetus inviso
vix mi ipse credens Thyniam atque Bithynos
liquisse campos et videre te in tuto.[4]

The Grotte di Cataulle is there; in "A Retrospect" Pound would insist that he "would much rather lie on what is left of Catullus' parlour floor and speculate the azure beneath it and the hills off to Salo and Riva with their forgotten gods moving unhindered amongst them, than discuss any processes and theories of art whatsoever" (*LE*, 9). And Flaminius, a Poundian enthusiasm which has not even caught on among Pound enthusiasts, had been there and "raved."[5] But it wasn't the literary associations which bound Ezra to Sirmio; it was the place itself.

He discovered it in the spring of 1910; he stumbled on it almost by accident, but it took, and he was to return to it perennially until the outbreak of the Great War and then again often thereafter. The first reverberations of the impact were in letters, but soon the ripple had extended into his early poetry, and it ultimately reached as far as *The Cantos*. The letters written from Sirmione in 1910 collected in the "Paige Carbons" at the Beinecke Library make interesting reading (though Paige, in making his selections for his edition of Pound's letters, ultimately chose to skip over 1910 entirely). They reveal that though Pound discovered Sirmione almost by accident, he did not feel that discovery to be in the least accidental; he felt it was intended: "I landed here not by my own intent or volition. I was set here by about as forceful a hand as could be imagined."[6] From the beginning Pound felt that Sirmione and the Lago di Garda were paradisical—he said as much in letters to his father and H.D. He installed himself in the Hotel Eden with the manuscript of *The Spirit of Romance*, with the expectation of a visit from the Shakespears within the month.[7]

What appeared paradisical to Pound about Lago di Garda was the quality of light. He wrote to H.D. that it couldn't be painted, that to catch it the artist would need to do it in stained glass; it was too brilliant, intense, and transparent for pigment.[8] In other words, nature in the *lago* approached or embodied the supernature of his visions, when things seemed to be lit from within, radiating light. In this sense, it was paradise. Not only was Garda lit from within, but, according to Pound, it even had lines in it, like the lead in stained glass.[9] The idea of landscape as stained glass would stay with him, even through the late cantos: "the sky's glass leaded with elm boughs" (107/761).

The early poems, from the period following his first acquaintance with the place, reflect Pound's feeling for it—"Blandula, Tenulla, Vagula," an address to his soul, insists on the *terreste* of this *paradis*, and speaks of the founding of a "cult" ("this rite"?) on the waves. In "The Flame," where we have already documented the presence of his "unofficial mysticism," Pound interjects into a visionary account an address to the Lago di Garda itself (Benacus), as a testament of supernatural reality:

Sapphire Benacus, in thy mists and thee
Nature herself's turned metaphysical,
Who can look on that blue and not believe? [P, 50]

Nature as testament, perhaps it was this that led Pound to *command* H.D. to journey to Garda.[10] Perhaps it was the geo-graphing of Sirmione itself. Sirmione is a long, slender peninsula; in a picture of it he drew for his father it looks suspiciously phallic—with the Hotel Eden sketched in out near the end.[11] Tempio indeed! If my suspicion seems fantastic, it should be remembered that Pound was certainly capable of usurping topographical usage to describe genitalia—hence the "concava vallis" of "Phanopoeia," the "By prong have I entered these hills" of 47 [47/238], and the "copulatrix / thy furrow" of 77 [77/470].[12] In any case, at Sirmione nature took on visionary colors for Pound, and this "sacred place" gravitated to Pound's ideogram of the erotic medium.

The references to Sirmione in *The Cantos* tend to be cryptic; the landscape is suggested by a phrase, usually in contexts where there is a vision in progress. From the early cantos, in 3:

    Gods float in the azure air,
Bright gods and Tuscan, back before dew was shed.
Light: and the first light, before ever dew was fallen.
Panisks, and from the oak, dryas,
And from the apple, mælid,
Through all the wood, and the leaves are full of voices,
A-whisper, and the clouds bowe over the lake,
And there are gods upon them . . . [3/11]

Kenner thinks the lake is Garda.[13] Its appearance here, in this light, this edenic, god-inhabited place complete with "elementals," is almost expected. In Canto 5 the context is even more explicitly visionary—if *spezzato*—and the reference to Garda correspondingly more occult. Again the light:

Iamblichus' light,
  the souls ascending,
Sparks like a partridge covey,
  Like the "ciocco", brand struck in the game.
"Et omniformis": Air, fire, the pale soft light.
Topaz I manage, and three sorts of blue;
  but on the barb of time. [5/17]

"Three sorts of blue" recalls the "triune azures" of "Blandula, Tenulla, Vagula," again, describing Garda from Sirmio. Ultimately the ear becomes atuned to descriptions of Sirmione, until the fragmentary references Pound makes to it in *The Cantos* register.[14] Of course, Sirmione and Garda are testament; they figure a state of mind evoked by an erotic medium, and we must read them that way, not so much as independent manifestations. Once the identification is made, we must ask how it functions in any particular passage.[15]

In 1930 Pound published a "Credo" in the journal *Front* (collected in *SP*, 53), an answer to Eliot's public questions as to just what Pound "believed." As a "Credo" it is decidedly light, but the position taken in it by Pound is a serious one, with the possible exception of the wish to build "a temple to Artemis in Park Lane" (*SP*, 53)—but even there, who knows? Pound, asked what he believes, offers "Given the material means I would replace the statue of Venus on the cliffs of Terracina."[16] The full force of the remark is clarified by cross-referencing it to one on his "A Visiting Card": "To replace the marble goddess on her pedestal at Terracina is worth more than any metaphysical argument" (*SP*, 320). This remark suggests that, besides prefering image to argument, Pound is serious at least about the value of such a (albeit creative) recovery. Pound had been there, seen the place, as the anecdotes in "Terra Italica" attest, where we find him admiring

the "grace of the well-curb of Terracina" (*SP*, 58), and recounting
that "You find in the sacristy at Terracina a small barrocco angel,
and the sacristan tells you that the bishop had it taken out of the
church because the peasants insisted on worshipping it" (*SP*, 60).
But Pound wants to replace the marble statue of Venus because
"aram nemus vult"—"this grove needs an altar."[17]

In *The Cantos* Terracina becomes a place where Pound's
erotic rite is performed, or ought to be peformed. In 39, for example, Pound juxtaposes two kinds of sexuality. Sex as indulgence,
stupefying rather than vivifying, is figured by Circe's thrall:

When I lay in the ingle of Circe
I heard a song. . . .
　Fat panther lay by me
Girls talked there of fucking, beasts talked there of eating,
All heavy with sleep, fucked girls and fat leopards,
Lions loggy with Circe's tisane,
Girls leery with Circe's tisane . . . [39/193]

This is the eroticism that issues in sleep—delay, one suspects, is
short in Circe's ingle. "Been to hell in a boat yet?"

"Right" sexuality is associated with Terracina, and the statue
of Venus, it seems, *has* been restored (or has not yet fallen):

To the beat of the measure
From star up to the half-dark
From half-dark to half-dark
　　Unceasing the measure
Flank by flank on the headland
　　with the Goddess' eyes to seaward
By Circeo, by Terracina, with the stone eyes
　　white toward the sea
With one measure, unceasing:
　　"Fac deum!" "Est factus."

.　.　.　.　.　.　.　.

Dark shoulders have stirred the lightning
A girl's arms have nested the fire,
Not I but the handmaid kindled
　　Cantat sic nupta
I have eaten the flame. [39/195–96]

Venus at Terracina, again and again in *The Cantos* she is figured with her stone eyes seaward, as an emblem of "this rite." In the Pisan Cantos, with the world in shambles, Pound looks forward to "the great healing":

> *I surrender neither the empire nor the temples*
> > *plural*
> *nor the constitution nor yet the city of Dioce*
> *each one in his god's name*
> *as by Terracina rose from the sea Zephyr behind her*
> > *and from her manner of walking*
> > > *as had Anchises*
> *till the shrine be again white with marble*
> *till the stone eyes look again seaward.* [76/434–35]

Terracina is, then, one of the temples of Pound's recital of mediumistic sexuality. At this point in the discussion it is possible to recognize the extreme coyness of Pound's treatment of Terracina in his *Guide to Kulchur* in a chapter entitled "The Proof of the Pudding." Pound wrote, "A live religion can not be maintained by scripture. It has got to go into effect repeatedly in the persons of the participants. I wd. set up the statue of Aphrodite again over Terracina. I doubt, to a reasonable extent, whether you can attain a living catholicism save after a greek pagan revival" (GK, 191). Here we do not have image against argument, but the Aphroditian rite itself against scripture. Pound is maintaining that a *live* religion depends on its participants—that the rite must be performed. By choosing Aphrodite at Terracina—in light of his other writings—Pound is occultly suggesting not any rite, but "this" erotic rite (actually, a rather startling proposal). In *The Cantos* we can recognize Terracina by its place names, and by the phrases "stone eyes to seaward" (and its variants) and "aram nemus vult." Yet we must not let the identification "Terracina" keep us from working out the function of the reference in every individual passage.

Eleusis and Montségur present rather different problems. Pound visited Montségur on a walking tour in Provence in 1919—Hugh Kenner has given us an account of it, right down to the

number of blisters (seven) T. S. Eliot suffered on his divagation
to view cave paintings.[18] It's a lively account, full of "gists and
piths." Kenner deftly sketches in the historical background, praises
Pound's peripatetic insight—seeing Ségur as "sacred to Helios"
years before a historian of Montségur, Fernand Niel, demonstrated
the place of the sun there.[19] But for my study, it is more important
to remember that Pound did not accept the official church accounts of Albigensian belief (Manichaean dualist), and thus rejected as well church explanations for the Albigensian Crusade
against Montségur. For Pound, "Les Albigeois" are a "problem of
history" (74/429):

And they went looking for Manicheans
And found, so far as I can make out, no Manicheans. [36/179]

Actual Manichaeans would have been worshippers of a cosmic
dualism, but Pound believed that the "servants of Amor" in
Provence—and at Montségur—were anything but dualists, as we
have seen, and that the church called them Manichaeans "as a
term of abuse." "For centuries if you disliked a man you called
him a Manichaean, as in some circles to-day you call him a Bol-
shevic to damage his earning capacity" (*LE*, 176). In a case like
this erudition may lead us astray; we must understand by Montségur what Pound tells us about it rather than what historians tell
us, or we will founder.[20] Pound intends by Montségur a temple of
the "servants of Amor."[21]

The case with Eleusis is similar if more complicated. There
have been some interesting studies done on the role of Eleusis in
Pound's work,[22] but they do not make a convincing case in the
matter of sources. It is not clear what Pound read about Eleusis,
and to gloss his work with something he may have read or clearly
did not read is a very risky procedure. It seems to me that Pound
knew very little about Eleusis, perhaps largely because there was
and is very little to know.[23] In such a situation we can expect that
Pound's (often happy) penchant for creative reading was likely
indulged; he is habitually not content to leave the blanks. Indeed,
Pound's reading of tradition is utterly idiosyncratic.[24] Pound does

not get vocal on the role of Eleusis until the 1930s, when he begins to make such assertions as "I believe that a light from Eleusis persisted throughout the middle ages and set beauty in the song of Provence and of Italy" (*SP*, 53). It is in "Terra Italica," the essay which gave us "For certain people the *pecten cteis* is the gate of wisdom" (*SP*, 56), that he presents his most complete exposition of the descent of wisdom through Eleusis to the "servants of Amor" in Provence. The argument runs, with some interlinear commentary, thus:

For all its inclusiveness . . . [Christianity] was for fifteen and more centuries troubled by heresies, mostly uninteresting and perhaps all of them traceable to some cult it had not included.
    One cult that it had failed to include was that of Eleusis.
    It may be arguable that Eleusinian elements persisted in the very early Church, and are responsible for some of the scandals. It is quite certain that the Church later emerges riddled with tendencies to fanaticism, with sadistic and masochistic tendencies that are in no way Eleusinian. [*SP*, 58]

The early scandals look back to the remark in "Psychology and Troubadours" which started the discussion in the "Servants of Amor" chapter of this study—to the debated practice of *virgines subintroductae.* He would remember the passage from Corinthians again in the Pisan Cantos:

    as in the advice to the young man to
breed and get married (or not)
        as you choose to regard it [83/534]

These are lines which must otherwise remain perplexing. Pound returns, in "Terra Italica," to his denigration of "stupid asceticism" as well. We are on familiar ground: "It is equally discernable upon study that some non-Christian and inextinguishable source of beauty persisted throughout the Middle Ages maintaining song in Provence, maintaining the grace of Kalenda Maya" (*SP*, 58). Pound here asserts a link, perhaps apostolical, perhaps simply in the "permanent basis in humanity," between an Eleusinian source and its maintenance in Provence, which he elaborates:

The usual accusation against the Albigeois is that they were Mani-
chaeans. This I believe after a long search to be pure bunkumb.
The slanderers feared the truth. . . .

   The best scholars do not believe that there were any Mani-
chaeans left in Europe at the time of the Albigensian Crusade. If
there were any in Provence they have at any rate left no trace in
troubadour art.

   On the other hand the cult of Eleusis will explain not only
general phenomena but particular beauties in Arnaut Daniel or in
Guido Cavalcanti. [SP, 58–59]

We have already seen that in Pound's recital Arnaut and Guido
were devotees of a visionary eroticism, which leaves little doubt
that Pound thought that the erotic rite, which found its way into
Provence and Italy and ultimately Pennsylvania, was performed in
the mysteries at Eleusis, a view which, if unpopular, is at least
considered in the scholarly literature on the subject.[25] And, as
mentioned earlier, Pound's enthusiasm for the *Sacerdotesse* pamphlet, a pamphlet largely focused on *hierogamia* at Eleusis and
elsewhere in the ancient world, as a guide to medieval *poetry*, provides substantial corroboration for this view.

   Eleusis stands then, genealogically, as a kind of grandparent
to Montségur. The mediumistic potentiality of sexuality, in these
two cases, was institutionalized as a cult. The decline of the two
cults, however, stemmed from different causes. Montségur was
crushed from without, in Pound's rendition, by a church that was
jealous of its followers and jealous of visions had without mortifi-
cation and a dark night of the soul: spiritual sour grapes. Eleusis,
Pound seems to have believed, died from within. As early as "Psychology and Troubadours" Pound displayed a sensitivity to the
potential for this kind of decline. "We should consider carefully
the history of the various cults or religions of orgy and ecstasy,
from the simpler Bacchanalia to the more complicated rites of
Isis and Dionysus—sudden rise and equally sudden decline. The
corruptions of their priesthoods follow, probably, the admission
thereto of one neophyte who was not properly 'sacerdos' "
(SR, 95). By the time of "Terra Italica" the "sacerdos" seems to

almost have become a matter of biology (the physiological dimension enters again). "The decline of the temples is I think understandable," he wrote. "Apart from bacteriological causes due to profanation the Eleusinian cult was obviously the most open to misunderstanding, the least possible to explain to barbarians" (*SP*, 59). Montségur and Eleusis, then, not only signal in *The Cantos* institutionalizations of "this rite," but also the vulnerability to decline such institutionalizations entail—thus linking up with the historical dimensions of *The Cantos*.

If "this rite" has its sacred places and its climes, it also has its seasons and its times. From *The Spirit of Romance* on Pound links the regeneration of spring to eroticism (clearly not an innovation, though the "visionary colours" of Pound's sexuality sets it to one side of the "vertu" of "swich licour" of Chaucer et al.). In "Psychology and Troubadours" Pound asserts that "Provençal song is never wholly disjunct from pagan rites of May Day" (*SR*, 90), though we should probably place as much emphasis on "pagan rites" as "May Day." What Pound understands by May Day is best glossed with his remarks in "The Phantom Dawn" (chapter 1 of *The Spirit of Romance*): "The *Pervigilium Veneris*, . . . is interesting for several reasons. It celebrates a Greek feast, which had been transplanted into Italy, and recently revived by Hadrian: the feast of Venus Genetrix, which survived as May Day" (*SR*, 18). Just as grain rites like Eleusis were fertility rites,[26] it is the fecundity of spring which draws Pound's eroticism to it as a magnet draws filings, and fecundity itself is the source of the natural abundance which lies at the heart of Pound's economic thinking (and herein is the link between two of Pound's major preoccupations). Neither interest should be slighted, for both visionary eroticism and economics inhere in Pound's treatment of fecundity and the spring that so obviously bodies it forth. But while seasonal references are important to this study, times of day seem more closely aligned to the Poundian ideogram for the erotic medium than times of the year.

The rite is performed at dawn; it is in this respect that "Helios" is "in some sense" a god of "this rite" (*SP*, 48). As I

have already suggested, from his juvenilia forward Pound devoted
a great deal of attention to dawn and the erotic *alba*. The dawn
song has, of course, an elaborate generical history. But Pound, here
as in the case of the spring song, has heightened the emotional
color to a visionary pitch (it is difficult even to guess how much of
the heightening descends from Pound's reading of the tradition
and how much is conscious addition). In *The Cantos*, dawn takes
on not only extraordinary emotional colors but theophanic significance in its conjunction with the erotic. Dawn is the moment
when the lovers "bust through," but if this is the metamorphic
moment, there are of course preliminaries. In a passage already
cited from Canto 39, the lovers seem to have spent the whole
night out—"From star up to the half-dark / From half-dark to
half-dark" (39/195)—but it's at dawn that the god "Est factus."
In the Lynx Canto, "We are here waiting the sun-rise" (79/491).
All this, "to enter the presence at sunrise . . ." (93/632). In the
notes to Rock-Drill, Pound is more explicit:

> @ dawn enter
>   presence of the gods
> &
>   revelation in sun orb
>   @ dawn—[27]

In the late cantos Pound becomes increasingly cryptic in his references to dawn as a time "to enter the presence." In a passage from
91, a passage which exhibits several of the radicals of the erotic
medium, Pound simply writes:

They who are skilled in fire [present knowers]

  shall read 旦 *tan, the dawn.*

Waiving no jot of the arcanum
    (having his own mind to stand by him). [91/615]

A good gloss on itself—"Waiving no jot of the arcanum"! But he
gets even more cryptic, page by page. In 97 it is down to

that at least a few should perceive this 旦 *tan* [97/677]

set off by extra space, followed significantly by a reference to
Arnaut. And again, in 97, with a link to grain rites and Demeter:

Luigi, gobbo, makes his communion with wheat grain
in the hill paths
at sunrise

ONE, *ten, eleven,* chi con me 且 *tan?* [97/679]

Those numbers remind us that we hardly know everything, though
something more·than what we knew before. There are probably
further occult links, to the "Memnon of the Dawn" (94/640) of
Apollonius (one of the heros of this text), and back to the problematical "great alley of Memnons" of Canto 17 (17/77).

Again from "Religio." Question: "To what other gods [besides
Apollo, Helios, Diana, and Aphrodite] is it fitting, in harmony or
in adjunction with these rites, to give incense?" Answer: "To Koré
and to Demeter" (*SP*, 48). Incense smells, perhaps, a little like
the inside of a church; does Pound really mean to suggest that
"this rite" is performed to incense? It does seem to run contrary to
the portrait of a hard modernist we are accustomed to, but I think
it is, nevertheless, probable. Pound, like the troubadours he ad-
mired, is not averse to taking over on behalf of Aphrodite certain
ritualistic elements from the church (nor is he averse to the
church borrowing from what he calls the religion of eros—
Godeschalk's "sequaire" for instance). Stock, in his biography
The Life of Ezra Pound, relates that William Carlos Williams, on
a 1910 visit to Pound in Kensington, saw a "photograph of a
woman with a lighted candle always burning before it."[28] Stock
suggests, correctly I think, that it was a picture of Bride Scratton,
and paraphrases from their unpublished correspondence that
Pound had written to her of "a lamp burning before a shrine."[29]
Some readers may be surprised to find Pound tolerating such practices, even if they were confined to 1910 and before—which they
are not—but though this may seem like treacle the impulse is really
no different than wanting to replace the statue of Aphrodite at
Terracina. Pound longs for ritual and institution—"To build a
dream over the world"[30] or "To build the city of Dioce whose
terraces are the colour of stars" (74/425).

In "Phanopoeia," an important early poem for our subject,

Pound speaks of "The smoke of incense" which "Mounts from the four horns of my bedposts" (*P*, 169), making of the bed a kind of altar, an impression which is strengthened by a line as late as Canto 92 (also in an implicated passage), "The four altars at the four coigns of that place" (92/619). In *The Cantos* the incense seems to be principally "olibanum" (frankincense) and to a lesser extent myrrh. Its offering has a propitiatory significance:

By olibanum, the polite salutation, the smoke sign;
  Do not pester the spirits. [63/624]

However, neither the bed nor the propitiation is always evident; sometimes it seems to be simply "fitting" (in another relevant passage):

οἱ χθόνιοι *myrrh and olibanum on the altar stone*
giving perfume . . . [90/608]

Although incense in *The* Cantos often accompanies "this rite," it is certainly not always mentioned nor is it only associated with mediumistic sexuality. Interestingly enough, it is very evident on the "Shelf of the lotophagoi" (20/93). Pound's position on "respectable dope smokers" is not, to me at least, an easy one to comprehend. It will be remembered that Pound included, in the catalogue of those who have seen, if darkly, a connection between their "sperm and their cerebration" (*NPL*, 182), which closed his "Translator's Postscript" to *The Natural Philosophy of Love*, the "dope-fiend" and that he concluded the catalogue with the ambiguous phrase "and probably with a basis of sanity" (*NPL*, 182). It seems possible that Pound thinks the "lotophagoi" at least approach some of the same experiences as those had by his mediumistic lovers. But there's a rub. The lotophagoi are not, like the lovers, vivified, but drift toward death, abandoning the world—very important world for Pound—of action:

        quiet, scornful,
Voce-profondo:
          "Feared neither death nor pain for this beauty;
If harm, harm to ourselves."

And beneath: the clear bones, far down,
Thousand on thousand. [20/93]

So, though Pound seems to acknowledge an experiential link, he thinks the access of the lotophagoi is poor, and the side effects unacceptable. All of which is meant as a cautionary note for those who would place an uncritical faith in the presence of incense as an indicator of an erotic rite. Even in a poem as difficult as *The Cantos* to determine what the context is, context is critically important.

In Canto 2 Pound identified olibanum as the incense of Bacchus [2/6–9], who brings with him, of course, the vines and wine. Olibanum, then, is associated both with Pound's ritual eroticism and with wine and the bacchanal. On the face of it this seems like an uneasy mélange. But in "Psychology and Troubadours," which as we saw was an essay brimming with cryptic references to visionary eroticism, Pound dissociated two kinds of religions, and that distinction will help us understand the double associations of olibanum. On the one hand, there are repressive religions, "the Mosaic or Roman or British Empire type," and on the other there are the "ecstatic religions" (*SR*, 95). He includes the bacchanalia as a simpler form of the latter, and it is to the latter that Pound's "unofficial mysticism" belongs as well, though presumably as a more complex form. The association of olibanum with both bacchic and erotic rites then does make theoretic sense—they are all under one umbrella, so to speak (Zagreus is probably with them under there).

The association, however, is not only theoretical; there is an experiential dimension as well. It seems to me extremely likely that wine was drunk in preparation for "this rite," a kind of nonnarcotic version of Circe's tisane (the parallel is extended: "not Circe / but Circe was like that"). Indeed, in the unpublished notes to Rock-Drill there is an unguarded line that reads "wine, copulation: a sacrament."[31] There is nothing that bald in the published *Cantos*, but the idea informs them. The closest thing to an epigram on the subject comes from Canto 27, "Xarites, born of Venus and wine" (27/131),[32] where "the graces" seem to have experiential and visionary significance; they seem to name felt-forms, as "swan's down ever" figures them. But if the references to actually drinking wine are few in *The Cantos*, especially to ritual drinking, the frequent presence of Bacchus, Dionysus-Zagreus, and attendant cats, does suggest a role for wine in "this rite"—as an "unchainer."[33]

Eyes populate *The Cantos*, increasingly in the later ones. Eyes, too, have a "radical" significance in Pound's ideogram for the erotic medium, though a full treatment of the subject would bulk so large that it cannot be attempted here, and much of the work has already been done.[34] Some aspects of the subject, however, particularly as they relate to the experiential dimension of Pound's eroticism, have not been adequately dealt with and must be here. It will be remembered that in his "Cavalcanti" essay Pound insisted that there was a distinction in kind between "normal" seeing, a matter of simple reception, and the extraordinary seeing of the lovers in "this rite"; in the latter case light is seen to proceed from the eyes of the lovers. Though Pound is explicit about this distinction in the notes to his cantos, in the published version it is largely implicit. In the following dissociation on artists, the distinction is in the "all":

all that Sandro knew, and Jacopo
   and that Velásquez never suspected
lost in the brown meat of Rembrandt
   and the raw meat of Rubens and Jordaens . . . [80/511]

To be able to read that "all" the reader must be conversant with Pound's "Cavalcanti," to understand that kinds of seeing are at issue, that the quality of the art is contingent.

In actual descriptions of eyes the reader's position is somewhat different. The kinds of seeing are embodied in the descriptions themselves, but the full significance of the descriptions is only apparent to those who understand the role of the two modes of seeing in Pound's thinking. Hence descriptions such as

> not Circe
> but Circe was like that
> coming from the house of smoothe stone
> "not know which god"
> nor could enter her eyes by probing
> the light blazed behind her
> nor was this from sunset. [106/754]

And the opposite case:

> The eyes holding trouble—
> no light
> ex profundis—
> naught from feigning. [Notes for 111/783]

Or, the light sometimes proceeds, but intermittently, *spezzato*:

> A match flares in the eyes' hearth,
> then darkness . . . [100/752]

In these cases it is simply a matter of seeing a logic in the descriptions, but there are leaps in this logic.

For example, Pound often describes eyes simply as sea-caves,
as the following lines from Canto 93 demonstrate:

> Risplende
> From the sea-caves
> degli occhi
> manifest and not abstract . . . [93/625]

Except for the sea-caves, this passage still moves within the ambit
of the ideas and vocabulary of Pound's "Cavalcanti," and the sea-
caves only restate the "degli occhi" (from the eyes). The identification, clear in this passage, is a little more difficult in others. Here
is another, also with light proceeding from the eyes:

> Such light is in sea-caves
> e la bella Ciprigna
> where copper throws back the flame
> from pinned eyes, the flames rise to fade
> in green air. [93/631]

Or again, from the same page:

There must be incognita
     and in sea-caves
          un lume pien' di spiriti,
               and of memories . . . [93/631]

Ultimately, the sea-caves in a canto like 17 may be eyes as well.[35]

This brings us to one of the oddest radicals in the whole ideo-gram of visionary eroticism—the role of Elizabeth in all this ("Miss Tudor"). In Canto 91 we find that the erotic medium has a political application! The principals are Sir Francis Drake and Queen Elizabeth:

Miss Tudor moved them with galleons
from deep eye, versus armada
from the green deep
               he saw it,
in the green deep of an eye:
     Crystal waves weaving together toward the gt/
               healing

.   .   .   .

Light & the flowing crystal
     never gin in cut glass had such clarity
That Drake saw the splendour and wreckage
               in that clarity
Gods moving in crystal
          ichor, amor

.   .   .   .

     That Drake saw the armada
          & sea caves

.   .   .   .

in the Queen's eye the reflection
     & sea wrack—
          green deep of the sea-cave
ne quaesaris. [91/611–12]

This *is* strange. Pound is not suggesting, of course, that there was a liaison between Drake and Elizabeth, though clearly this

passage is invested with a good many of the motifs we have come
to associate with Pound's lovers: the flowing crystal, the gods, the
gin in the cut glass recalling the glass under water of the "Cavalcanti," the "ne quaesaris" looking back to "Psychology and Troubadours,"[36] and the eyes or sea-caves. I think he is suggesting that
there are two "charged poles" in the relationship, that Drake's de-
votion is such that Elizabeth can perform a mediumistic role for
him without the poles being at "first in contact" (SR, 93). This is
closer to the humanized Christ in the beds of the virgins in
Godeschalk's "sequaire" or to Guido's "pastorella."

Elizabeth, in this recital of history, serves as a medium to introduce Drake to the "radiant world," but additionally, her eyes
serve as a kind of crystal ball in which Drake is able to foresee the
disaster which would overtake the Spanish Armada—it allows him
to see the future (there is a subject rhyme here with ἐλέναυς—the
destroyer of ships of Canto 2—but Drake sees past sea-wrack to
the "gt/healing" when he gazes on Elizabeth's eye). Drake himself is freed of doubt, he is "ne quaesaris"—"he asked not / nor
wavered" (91/612). He is proof against the question "Yet, having
seen the armada / turn back?" (92/621). This is, perhaps, the
political significance of attenuated eroticism, but Pound seems to
take the matter even further: the struggle seems to be understood
as the strength of eros against the strength of the world, or perhaps even the strength of sensitivity over against the powers of
"desensitization"—"versus armada." In Pound's polarized history
it is a rare victory in the tide:

> 25 *hundred years desensitization*
> 　　*2 thousand years, desensitization*
> *After Apollonius, desensitization*
> 　　*& a little light from the borders* . . . [92/621–22]

That the tide is so overwhelming suggests a little skepticism on
Pound's part about the ultimate efficacy of Amor in politics.

Before passing on from the subject of eyes, those eyes which
appear to Pound in his tent at Pisa must at least be mentioned.
They have already received what to me seems an admirable gloss
in the essay "The '*Tre Donne*' of the Pisan Cantos," by Wendy

Stallard Flory.[37] Flory, concentrating on the biographical dimension of the Pisan Cantos, demonstrates satisfactorily that on that level the three sets of eyes which appear to Pound are those of Dorothy Pound, Olga Rudge, and Bride Scratton,[38] though in the process she slights the mythological and historical echoes of the "tre donne." From Canto 81:

> *there came new subtlety of eyes into my tent,*
> *whether of spirit or hypostasis,*
> > *but what the blindfold hides*
> *or at carneval*
> > > > *nor any pair showed anger*
> > *Saw but the eyes and stance between the eyes,*
> *colour, diastasis,*
> > *careless or unaware it had not the*
> > *whole tent's room*
> *nor was place for the full* Eἰδὼς
> *interpass, penetrate*
> > > *casting but shade beyond the other lights*
> > > > *sky's clear*
> > > > *night's sea*
> > > > *green of the mountain pool*
> > > > *shone from the unmasked eyes in half-mask's space.*
> *What thou lovest well remains,*
> > > > > *the rest is dross*
> *What thou lov'st well shall not be reft from thee*
> *What thou lov'st well is thy true heritage*
> *Whose world, or mine or theirs*
> > > > *or is it of none?*
> *First came the seen, then thus the palpable*
> > *Elysium, though it were in the halls of hell.* [81/520–21]

The first thing which must be understood about this passage is that this vision proceeds from memory, is in fact the best example of what Pound means when he quotes Cavalcanti's "dove sta memoria." There is a prehistory—the erotic rites have already been performed. Pound just gives us the phrase, and leaves it to the

cognoscenti to remember the context in his "Cavalcanti," leaves it
to "present knowers" to remember its significance there:

> nothing matters but the quality
> of the affection—
> in the end—that has carved the trace in the mind
> dove sta memoria . . . [76/457]

And a few pages earlier:

> . . . that certain images be formed in the mind
>   to remain there
>   formato locho
>   Arachne mi porta fortuna
> to remain there, resurgent ΕΙΚΟΝΕΣ [74/446]

    D. S. Carne-Ross, in his admirable essay "The Music of a Lost
Dynasty," has dealt with these same passages,[39] but it is not clear
to me that he recognizes in the phrase *dove sta memoria* more
than simple memory: "Wherever the quality of the affection—
Aphrodite—is strong enough to carve a trace in the mind, the past
is preserved and its content, its images, rise up again and are renewed like the moon—Artemis—that renews herself each month."[40]
This is to reduce the *quality* of affection to the *quantity* of affection, and the "Cavalcanti" essay insists on *qualitative* distinctions.
Let's examine Pound's translation of the stanza of Cavalcanti's
"Donna Mi Prega" in which the phrase *dove sta memoria* occurs
in an effort to determine the quality of memory involved:

> In memory's *locus taketh he his state* [dove sta memoria]
> *Formed there in manner as a mist of light* [diafan]
> *Upon a dusk that is come from Mars and stays.*
> *Love is created, hath a sensate name,*
> *His modus takes from soul, from heart his will;*
> *From form seen doth he start, that, understood,*
> *Taketh in latent intellect—*[possible intelleto]
> *As in a subject ready—*
>   *place and abode,*
> *Yet in that place it ever is unstill,*
> *Spreading its rays,* . . . [risplende][41]

In prehistory, then, in the erotic encounter, the lover sees the beloved, she is the "form seen" from which love "starts," but this is not the form that remains "where memory liveth." This form is transformed in the passage into the "latent intellect" (*possible intelleto*), where she becomes Amor, a "diafan," unstill and "risplende." Ultimately the "form seen" is left behind entirely, in favor of the *diafan* in the lover's own mind (*possible intelleto*):

Who well proceedeth, form not seeth,
            following his own emanation.
There, beyond colour, essence set apart,
In midst of darkness light light giveth forth
Beyond all falsity, worthy of faith, alone . . . [LE, 157]

The memory or vision of the eyes serves as a mantram to get Pound in touch, again, with the radiant world—in the absence of any present lover. It is this process which makes it possible for Pound to know "Elysium" in Pisa, "though it were in the halls of hell"—the mediumistic erotic experience has formed an icon in the mind, which can be "resurgent" when the beloved is not present. The language of "Donna Mi Prega" and the "Cavalcanti" essay is *always* loaded in *The Cantos*, bringing with it pieces of "this rite," and implying, by synecdoche, the entire ideogram. "Risplende," "unstill," "diafan," "dove sta memoria," and so on, and their variants, all function in this way. We should be prepared to see the link between sexuality and the *diafan* in a passage like:

nor is it for nothing that the chrysalids mate in the air
            color di luce
green splendour and as the sun thru pale fingers. [74/432]

And phrases like ". . . nor is this yet *atasal*" and "tangibility by no means *atasal*" (76/458–59) from the Pisan Cantos, glossed by "the word is said to mean 'union with god' and to come from the writings of Avicenna, the Mohammedan physician and philosopher" in Edwards and Vasse,[42] should not send us scurrying into the stacks, but again to "Cavalcanti," where Pound—once again debunking intellectualizations of the "Donna Mi Prega"—wrote "I do not, in the canzone, smell 'ittisâl,' Sufi doctrine of union"

(*LE*, 186). In saying *not atasal* Pound is not saying nothing but
something else, and that something else can be glossed from
Pound's essay to be *union,* but with woman rather than God, leading to paradisical states of mind.

The foregoing, of course, is not a complete compilation of the
"external" radicals which bear on our subject, but as an annotated
listing it is sufficient to enable the careful reader to identify a good
many of the passages in *The Cantos* where the erotic medium is
implicated and detailed enough to provide a purchase on the particular force of any given reference. With the addition of the "subjective" radicals, to be discussed in the next chapter, few implicated passages of any length will remain occult enough to escape
detection. And detection, in a case like this where there is a great
deal of authorial indirection—not to say downright obfuscation—is
the better part of understanding (intellectual understanding, to
honor a Poundian stricture). Scholarship can go no further; at
some point, as Pound pointed out, the mysteries are self-defending.

The Cantos: Third Assay

*We might come to believe that the thing that matters in art is a
sort of energy, something more or less like electricity or radioac-
tivity, a force transfusing, welding, and unifying. A force rather
like water when it spurts up through very bright sand and sets it
in swift motion.* Pound, "The Serious Artist"

*The water whirls up the bright
sand in the spring's mouth*
Pound, Canto 4

*Eyes brown topaz,
Brookwater over brown sand*
Pound, Canto 29

Toward the end of Canto 78 Pound returns to his "tre donne," to
the prelude of vision felt in the tent at Pisa:

> *that presage*
> *in the air*
> *which means that nothing will happen that will
> be visible to the sargeants*
> *Tre donne intorno alla mia mente* . . . [78/483]

Read: Something will happen, but it will be invisible to the ser-
geants. It will be invisible, because as Pound says earlier in the
Pisan Cantos, "the drama is wholly subjective" (74/430). The subjective dimension of Pound's erotic medium, that is, the vision as
it is experienced, has its own discrete set of "radicals." Pound ar-

ranges them, choosing from among them, repeating them, creating resonances, and juxtaposes them, as if working through the permutations, searching for an unattainable equation that will "write Paradise" (120/803).[1] In this chapter I will try to reconstruct the most important of these radicals, to piece together the fragments which Pound has dispersed throughout his work, in the belief that a survey of the whole will make the fragments more easily identifiable. Procedurally, then, I am working as in the preceding chapter, but I am turning my attention from external topics to subjective ones. I will avoid, where possible, repetition of matter dealt with in earlier chapters, again counting on the reader's memory; some recapitulations, however, will be necessary.

In his "Religio" Pound makes a dissociation which is useful for categorizing the varieties of his "theophanic" experiences:

> *In what manner do gods appear?*
> *Formed and formlessly.*
> *To what do they appear when formed?*
> *To the sense of vision.*
> *And when formless?*
> *To the sense of knowledge.*
> *May they when formed appear to anything save the sense of* vision?
> *We may gain a sense of their presence as if they were standing behind us.*
> *And in this case they may possess form?*
> *We may feel that they do possess form.* [SP, 47–48]

Our interest is in the "formed," both as it appeals to the sense of vision and as it is felt, and—because the apparitions are subjective—in the effect of the attendant "states of mind" on the sense of sight. The "formed" as it appears to the "sense of vision," the properly visionary element of Pound's "unofficial mysticism," will be treated first. But this, too, requires some subdividing—the light which proceeds from the eye (discussed in detail earlier), the light around the body, the crystalline, and visions as pictures, the gods.

The light around the body is difficult to put a name on, because Pound, though he often describes it rarely names it, and when he does he is inconsistent; and to put a name on it, such as *augoeides*, aura, or subtle body, is to color our response to his descriptions. But whatever it's to be called, it is understood that it is the erotic encounter which allows the lover to see it. In the early poetry this light is usually described as a flame; later, Pound came to prefer cooler adjectives. In "Phanopoeia" he uses both:

The folding and lapping brightness
Has held in the air before you.
You have perceived the leaves of the flame. [P, 169]

If this seems like Swinburnian early Pound, the image of the first two lines stayed with him to the end, perhaps coming into slightly clearer focus. In Canto 113:

That the body is inside the soul—
> *the lifting and folding brightness*
> *the darkness shattered,*
>> *the fragment.* [113/788–89]

Here Pound describes this luminous envelope which he sees surrounding the body, and also names it, following Plotinus by Pound's own avowal (98/690 and elsewhere), the soul. But this label, like *augoeides* and the others, doesn't quite want to stick. In the "Notes for CXI" we read:

Soul melts into air,
> *anima into aura,*
>> *Serenitas.* [Notes for 111/783]

In this passage, it seems that soul (anima), when it becomes visible in the air around the body, becomes aura. Are the terms equivalent? It seems to me that the usage is not so much sloppy as provisional, always deferring to the precedence of experience: "I have seen what I have seen" (2/9).

But perhaps Pound is not as synthetic as he seems in his assignment of names to experiences; perhaps, as I suggested earlier, Pound is distinguishing among "subtle vehicles" in *The Cantos*, and images like "flame," "light," and "crystal" refer to different stages of a continuing experience. In Rock-Drill, at least, there is evidence to support these hypotheses: "that the body of light come forth / from the body of fire" (91/610); "& from fire to crystal / via the body of light" (91/615). I do not feel that I can rule out the possibility that the progression which informs these passages might be inherent in Pound's work fairly early on, though if it is the distinction is difficult to see, in that "the body of light" and "the body of fire" seem almost interchangeable there. The distinction does remind one that in "Psychology and Troubadours" Pound wrote, *as a metaphor* for the role of delay in producing vision from eros, "no scientist would be so stupid as to affirm that heat produced light" and "the electric current gives light where it meets resistance" (*SR*, 94–97). It is possible, then, that "the body of fire" figures simple electric attraction, the raw material which is then sublimated into "the body of light" by delay.

I put forth this hypothesis merely to pose the problem. What is clear is that both flames and light contribute to the ideogram of the erotic medium in *The Cantos*. The pertinence of flames is evident in this passage from 21:

And after that hour, dry darkness
Floating flame in the air, gonads in organdy,
Dry flamelet, a petal borne in the wind.
Gignetei kalon. [21/99]

And this, from 39:

Dark shoulders have stirred the lightning
A girl's arms have nested the fire . . . [39/196]

Flames, obviously, do suggest heat, and Pound pairs that with dryness, perhaps to distinguish it from the liquidity of his descriptions of light—"as light into water compenetrans," he says in Canto 100 (100/722), emphasizing how it looks, "Light *compenetrans* of the spirits" (91/611), he says in Canto 91, to establish the visionary resonance.[2] And, varying the formula a little in 93, "un lume pien' di spiriti" (93/631).

The liquidity of the light which the lover sees around or before the body of the beloved is figured in many ways, perhaps principally in the verbs—it flows, falls, and pours. And just as anima

seems capable of metamorphosing into aura, and flame into light,
the liquid light seems to become—again by implicit progression—
"crystal," as in the following passage from 4:

Thus the light rains, thus pours, e lo soleills plovil
The liquid and rushing crystal
*   beneath the knees of the gods.* [4/15]

The crystal, itself, is fluid, and seems at times to be particularly
visible around the hands:

no cloud, but the crystal body
*   the tangent formed in the hand's cup*
*   as live wind in the beech grove*
*   as strong air amid cypress . . .* [76/457]

If this crystal body is "fluid,"[3] the preceding quotation suggests we
are to understand fluidity rather than fluids—the fluidity of air.
The crystal body is ethereal; it is "the crystal body of air" (107/
762). This ethereal body has the visual quality of crystal in its
luminosity, and moves like a liquid, thus "the glass under water"
of the "Cavalcanti" essay and the "Light & the flowing crystal /
never gin in cut glass had such clarity" of 91 (91/611). These are
simply visual descriptions.

The crystal body, though it is ethereal, does not appeal solely
to vision, but to touch as well, as this passage from 76 demonstrates
(again, the hands):

spiriti questi? personae?
*   tangibility by no means atasal*
*   but the crystal can be weighed in the hand . . .* [76/459]

And where a liquid can only take the form of the vessel that contains it, Pound's crystal is *formal*, takes shapes. This is, finally, perhaps the best explanation of the "Sub Mare" tent effect, discussed
earlier:

*   and saw then, as of waves taking form,*
As the sea, hard, a glitter of crystal,
And the waves rising but formed, holding their form. [23/109]

As the crystal bodies of the lovers extend over them, fluid, moving, taking the shape of a wave, the lovers feel themselves "sub mare." It flows above, "the crystalline, as inverse of water, / clear over rock-bed" (76/457). This is the wave that rises over Tyro when she is taken by Poseidon:

> *Lithe turning of water,*
> > *sinews of Poseidon,*
> *Black azure and hyaline,*
> > *glass wave over Tyro,*
> *Close cover, unstillness,*
> > *bright welter of wave cords . . .* [2/9–10]

But the shapes the crystalline is capable of assuming are not limited to waves; there are "crystal funnels" (90/608 and 100/716) which lead out of Erebus—and which suggest we ought not be too mechanical about our understanding of Pound's "vorticism"— crystal rivers (re Guido), acorns (re his "Postscript"), and the "great ball of crystal." The crystal light is so tangible it's "almost solid" (95/644), so solid you could almost build with it (94/642).

For Pound, to enter the crystal fluid is to be renewed, healed; the resonance is almost medical:

> *She enters protection,*
> > *the great cloud is about her,*
> *She has entered the protection of crystal . . .* [91/611]

The—crystalline—experience, naturally, had for Pound a permanent basis in humanity, and he never stopped insisting on the current possibilities of access:

> *A lost kind of experience?*
> > *scarcely,*
> *O Queen Cytherea,*
> > *che'l terzo ciel movete.* [91/617]

Ultimately, Pound winnows his readers according to their ability to experience (not to know about) the "GREAT CRYSTAL" (91/611):

> *I have brought the great ball of crystal;*
> > *who can lift it?*
> *Can you enter the great acorn of light?* [116/795]

The status of the gods in *The Cantos* poses a difficult question for any reader of Pound's long poem, a question I cannot hope to answer here but which I must, nevertheless, address, if only to place the "visions of the gods" which occur in *The Cantos* in a context. In "The Child's Guide to Knowledge" Pound held that "a god is an eternal state of mind"—a provocative but cryptic formulation—and insisted that these states of mind might or might not manifest as "form" (*SP*, 47). It is evident, I think, that a good many of the references to the gods in *The Cantos* do not figure the visionary perception of divine form, but rather "an eternal state of mind." Nowhere in his published work, however, is Pound very explicit about the content of these states of mind as they appear in *The Cantos* under the names of "gods." But in a draft of Canto 25 Pound left enough to at least provide us with an intimation of what his own subjective pantheon was like:

the five gods, into the νΟΥΣ *of Apollo;*
   the framer, the maker of form;
Kypris, the [?], cohesion,
   the sister of Phoebos, the swift footed
                Artemisa,
and with them Zagrus, the unchainer,
and Pan, to bios . . .[4]

Of course, we must beware of supposing that these states of mind are ordinary, for Pound insists that while gods figure "an eternal state of mind" all "durable" states of mind are not gods (*SP*, 47). We must imagine at the very least an extraordinary intensity, but I think we should really understand a qualitatively abnormal state of mind. In a related statement on myth, Pound characterized the engendering experience as being, vis-à-vis normal experience, "nonsense" (*LE*, 437), and the same extraordinary quality probably inheres in the "states of mind" he calls gods.

A good many of the references to the gods in *The Cantos*, of course, may be literary allusions, though perhaps not simply literary, in that Pound's reading of myth was certainly informed by his own views on its experiential roots. Pound seemingly believed that the appearance of a god in a Greek text served as a notation for an extraordinary experience (*SR*, 93), which suggests that *Ox-*

ford Classical Dictionary definitions are likely to be counterfeit
currency if passed uncritically into *The Cantos*. The degree to
which Pound's use of classical and other more exotic pantheons is
idiosyncratic is a subject which deserves a study. Provisionally, as a
safe working hypothesis, I would venture that it is very idiosyncratic.

If some of the references to the gods in *The Cantos* figure un-
formed states of mind, if some are "mythic" in Pound's sense, and
some are literary illusions, still others are strictly visionary—the
gods are seen. For instance, "Diana," in 4:

> *the air, air,*
> *Shaking, air alight with the goddess* . . . [4/14]

In Canto 3, "Bright gods and Tuscan" float "in the azure air"
(3/11). Indeed, when the gods are "seen," it is generally in the
air, or "the timeless air." But not always; sometimes, at least, they
appear in the crystal body (really, almost as in a crystal ball)

> *formal and passing within the [crystal] sphere: Thetis,*
> *Maya, 'Αφροδίτη* . . . [76/459]

Aphrodite appears here because whatever status (plural) the gods
may have in *The Cantos*, whether they are felt or seen, they are
usually "called up" through the mediumistic potentialities of sexuality, and very often appear in passages along with other radicals
of Pound's ideogram of the erotic medium.

Pound's assertion in his "Religio" that "a god" may appeal to
other senses than vision, that we "may gain a sense of their presence as if they were standing behind us," encourages the suspicion
that this sensing of the gods may well have one or even several
manifestations in *The Cantos*, as the properly visionary does.
There are a number of candidates. The "tree motif," already discussed at some length, comes to mind; it certainly figures felt-
experience rather than seen-experience and it is certainly linked
to the ideogram of Pound's mediumistic sexuality, but Pound ac-
cords it mythic rather than divine status, though that distinction
in Pound's work often blurs. He certainly thinks Ovid's *Meta-*

morphoses is a holy book (GK, 299 and elsewhere), and Daphne's story is recounted there. Another candidate, I think, is the presence of cats which inhabit the long poem and a few of Pound's earlier lyrics, though it must be admitted at once that this is speculation and if the cats are a felt-presence this in no way contradicts their emblematic function as attendants of Zagreus. The status of the cats may be multiple, and it is certainly difficult to pin them down. It is very clear, nonetheless, that they are related to sexuality in *The Cantos*; though their association with Zagreus may be sufficient to explain their presence, a passage like "Lifeless air become sinewed" (2/8) in the sea-change passage redacted out of Ovid in Canto 2 does suggest the kind of felt form which the "Religio" passage leads us to expect. The difficulty of identifying these cats is compounded by a letter Dorothy Shakespear wrote to Pound on 26 December 1913, in which she reported that "I saw the Bl. Panther lying on my hearth rug one night when I was wakeful with the most alarming distinctness. He was stretched out on his side with his long tail round his hind ankles. I was quite alarmed! And another night I felt him sitting stiff up by the fire."[5] Here *the* "Bl. Panther" seems now apparitional, now "felt," but in any case more than a literary conceit. In *End to Torment*, H.D. makes it clear that she thinks it is Pound himself who is metamorphosed into a lynx in Canto 79,[6] but this is manifestly too simple. The difficulty here is typical; the status of a good many of Pound's statements are difficult of determination. Indeed, it very well may be that their status is not one that admits of explicit categorization.[7]

A "luminosity in vision" is seemingly attendant on all the extraordinary states of mind Pound claims for his lovers. This luminosity is not confined to apparitions, but passes over into the world at large, not only to the natural world but to the man-made world as well. In the end, the gist out of Erigena says it best, writ large: "OMNIA, QUAE SUNT, LUMINA SUNT" ("all things that are are lights" [74/429]). But in *The Cantos* this luminosity is, by and large, not treated so metaphysically—a metaphysicality which sits uneasily with Pound—but is rather simply present in luminous objects. That such objects populate *The Cantos* is apparent to all of its readers, and the role of luminosity in Pound's ideogram has been touched on several times already in this study. It is pineal seeing, in Pound's physiology.

It is unnecessary, then, to demonstrate the presence of "luminosity in vision" in Pound's work, but, in Pound's phrase, we should realize that it is this luminosity which accounts for many of the "particular beauties" of his poetry. From the Lynx Canto:

This fruit has a fire within it,
            Pomona, Pomona
No glass is clearer than are the globes of this flame
what sea is clearer than the pomegranate body
            holding the flame?
            Pomona, Pomona

.   .   .   .

    When the pomegranate is open and the light falls
half thru it . . . [79/490]

Or again:

"Ηλιος is come to our mountain
there is a red glow in the carpet of pine spikes. [79/492]

What the reader needs to remember is that there is more to this luminosity than "effects of light," that the description of luminous objects in *The Cantos* describes both the objects and the erotically induced state of mind that produces "luminosity in vision." This is particularly true in passages where other "radicals" of the erotic medium are also present, which is certainly the case in the Lynx Canto from which the preceding lines are taken.

There is a visionary world, by Pound's account, a world in which all things are lights, where luminous subtle bodies billow around physical bodies, where gods are seen, and the unseen sinews the air. For certain people, Pound insists, this world is opened by the mediumistic potential of sexuality to put the lover in touch. But if the *pecten cteis* is the gate to this world, the contact is not permanent. In this life, Pound concedes, there is no permanent residence in the visionary world. It is this intermittent quality of the contact that I have called, choosing one word from among the many Pound uses, *spezzato*.[8] But no matter what the word, the flickering quality is always the same (the basis in experience, one expects). One chain link:

> *Le Paradis n'est pas artificiel*
> *but spezzato apparently* . . . [74/438]

To:

Le Paradis n'est pas artificiel
>> *but is jagged,*
For a flash,
>> *for an hour.* [92/620]

To:

"non sempre" (in the 3rd of Convivio)
or as above stated "jagged." [93/626][9]

It would not be pushing too hard, I think, to see another statement of this flickering quality in Pound's use of the Greek words γλαύξ and γλαυκῶπις. Of course, as Hugh Kenner documents in his *Pound Era*, Pound's understanding of this word was informed by his reading of Allen Upward.[10] But Kenner stops before asking what Pound might have been seeing in Upward's speculations—in *The Cantos* γλαύξ rhymes with *spezzato*, it is the flickering quality of theophany:

> *no vestige save in the air*
> *in stone is no imprint and the grey walls of no era*
>> *under the olives*
>> *saeculorum Athenae*
>> γλαύξ, γλαυκῶπις,
>>> *olivi*
> *that which gleams and then does not gleam*
>> *as the leaf turns in the air* . . . [74/438]

We should not forget that the *glaukopis* which Upward is glossing is an adjective applied to the eyes of "the *goddess* Athene."[11]

Glaukopis, "that which gleams and then does not gleam," informs a passage from Canto 21 which also records the intermittent nature of Pound's vision, though the word is suppressed:

In the crisp air,
        the discontinuous gods;
Pallas, young owl in the cup of her hand,
And, by night, the stag runs, and the leopard,
Owl-eye amid pine boughs. [21/99]

Both *spezzato* and *glaukopis* figure the "discontinuity" of the gods: "the vision, flitting / And fading at will" (5/17). Pound doesn't lament this discontinuity; he simply accepts it as a given of existence—"non sempre" short of Paradise. What Pound does seem to fear is the uneasy position this discontinuousness places these experiences in vis-à-vis "the truth." It is a problem, one he addressed covertly, I believe, in the following passage from *Guide to Kulchur:* "Certain objects are communicable to a man or woman only 'with proper lighting', they are perceptible in our own minds only with proper 'lighting', fitfully and by instants" (GK, 295).

Concluding Informally

To communicate and then stop,
that is the law of discourse.
Pound, Canto 80

In the end, if a study like this is pursued too far it must founder.
In taking as *ultimo ratio* experience, Pound's experience of what
he designates mystery, the scholar must ultimately find that experience is for participants; the scholar remains at a distance, in
the "outer courts." It is a perilous distance; those who impugn
scholarship will hardly, in this case, be able to resist the label
"voyeur." Pound, I think it should be admitted, would probably
not have cast a favorable eye on this project. Indeed, while reading the "Savoir Faire" chapter of *Guide to Kulchur*, in a passage
devoted to Eleusis (which stands like a bright emblem of Pound's
erotic medium), I felt myself addressed, and chastened:

> *prose is* NOT *education but the outer courts of the same. Beyond*
> *its doors are the mysteries. Eleusis. Things not to be spoken save*
> *in secret.*
>
> *The mysteries self-defended, the mysteries that* can *not be*
> *revealed. Fools can only profane them. The dull can neither pene-*
> *trate the secretum nor divulge it to others.* [GK, 144–45]

If this is "savoir faire," my study is, perhaps, a very extensive "faux
pas." But, in my own defense, I have tried to honor the integrity
of experience, and the mystery. If I have spoken in public, it *is* in
the belief that what ought not be revealed cannot be revealed.
This study remains in the "outer courts"; I have been content to

insist that for Pound there is a "place" beyond the doors, that in both the early poetry and in *The Cantos* the erotic mystery is there, not explicitly, but actuating what we do see.

And times have changed; the largely Victorian audience of Pound's early work has long been supplanted, and a poet of Pound's views on the erotic would not, today, really need to "shield himself from persecution" by having recourse to indirection, though there might be those "slanderers" Pound felt his elect had always been prey to. Certainly there is room for misunderstanding, but surely a right understanding of Pound's eroticism is preferable to the charge of simple philandering that the externals of "this rite" have exposed him to?

Pound himself, as my reliance on his work makes clear, is my chief witness. In essays like "Psychology and Troubadours" and "Cavalcanti," he baited too tempting a hook to cast into a pond full of scholars without the expectation of a strike. Indeed, in all his works which bear on mediumistic sexuality, Pound is undeniably coy, beckoning us forward even as he draws the curtain. And there is something inescapably public about this man Pound; he is a poet of such large gestures that even his covering up approaches exhibition (every exhibitionist finds his voyeur!).

H.D.'s *End to Torment* reveals, among other things, that even in that maple tree in Pennsylvania that detained us in the introduction there was an element of the public—the "inevitable parent."[1] The "fiery moment" should not be so visible, perhaps, but Pound and H.D., in their green days, seemed always to be too visible, "caught 'in the very act' you might say."[2] On another occasion their "fiery kisses" were "enough to draw an audience. The school girls, it was discovered, had assembled on the balcony above. . . . anyhow, the girls had had their peepshow."[3] Theirs was a love "in the arena" and often before a disapproving crowd. No figure as public as the later Pound can avoid an audience, and Pound hardly tried to hide from it. His amours, from H.D. to "Undine," are scarcely secret; and though in this study I have tried to steer clear of any untoward interest in the biographical dimension of Pound's preoccupations with mediumistic sexuality, it is not because there isn't a good deal of information, but because the biography is less illuminating than the prose when it comes to deciphering the poetry, and because I think that what has remained private of Pound's "private life" is not for me to discover.

I found at the Pound Archive in the Beinecke Library that the researcher is not given full access to the Pound collection, particularly when the personal dimension of Pound's career is in question. So even if I had chosen to pursue the biography there would have been many lacunae; perhaps in the future there will be a fuller disclosure, and what is left of Pound's privacy will enter the public domain. I expect, at that time, that some details of this study may stand in need of revision, but I can not believe that any biographical disclosure will call into question its main outlines.

I have tried to read Pound as I found him in his works, and what I have found is that the Pound(s) of the critics is more the hardheaded modern than the man. Of course, Pound would have maintained that there was nothing softheaded about his visionary eroticism, that it was firmly grounded in the world of fact, and that our "rank folly" response derives from either a failure of experience or a refusal to admit anything which does not conform to our cultural syllogisms about the nature of reality. By focusing on the visionary side of Pound I have, of course, not presented a balanced account of the man either. I have not forgotten that the lion's share of Pound's mature output is devoted to the "diagnosis" of ugliness rather than the "cult of Beauty" (and I realize I am not alone in my emphasis). But the scholar must focus—"communicate and then stop."

Notes

A Maple Tree in Pennsylvania

1   H.D., *End to Torment, A Memoir of Ezra Pound*, with the poems from "Hilda's Book" by Ezra Pound, ed. Norman Holmes Pearson and Michael King (New York: New Directions, 1979). In his foreword Michael King ventures that this book was "twenty years in the making," but really it was only a few months in the making, and twenty years in the waiting. It was written during a period of convalesence in Kusnacht, Switzerland. Composed as a journal, the first entry is dated 7 March 1958, and the last 13 July of the same year. It was written at the instigation of Norman Holmes Pearson, H.D.'s literary adviser and friend to both H.D. and Pound, and under the intermittent prodding of her doctor at Kusnacht, Erich Heydt. The dates of composition span the weeks leading up to and immediately following Pound's release from St. Elizabeths; it was a time of considerable journalistic furor on the subject of Pound, and it seems no one contemplated the publication of *End to Torment* in that climate: not Pearson, H.D., or Pound. The delay in publication probably also reflects a certain delicacy about the principals, a delicacy Michael King continues on behalf of the living, declining by omission to identify Pound's "spirit love" of his St. Elizabeths years beyond "Undine."

2   Ibid., p. 12.

3   For a useful recital of Pound and H.D. in Pennsylvania see Michael King, "Go, Little Book: Ezra Pound, Hilda Doolittle and 'Hilda's Book,' " *Paideuma* 10 (Fall 1981): 347–60. However, King's commonsensical approach does not do justice to how extraordinary their relationship was: a lifelong instigation for both of them. See, too, H.D.'s *HERmione* (New York: New Directions, 1981), an autobiographical novel concerned, in large part, with H.D.'s broken engagement with Pound (who figures as George Lowndes).

4   H.D., *End to Torment*, p. 55.

5   Ibid., p. 46.

6   Ibid., pp. 10–11.

7   Ibid., pp. 18–19.

8 Ibid., p. 24.
9 Ezra Pound, *The Cantos* (New York: New Directions, 1975), p. 620.
10 H.D., *End to Torment*, p. 19.
11 Ibid., p. 35.
12 Ezra Pound, *The Spirit of Romance* (New York: New Directions, 1968), p. 97.
13 H.D., *End to Torment*, p. 28.
14 Bound up with *End to Torment*.
15 H.D., *End to Torment*, pp. 37–38.
16 Ibid., p. 17.
17 Ibid., p. 34.
18 Ibid., p. 39.
19 Ibid., p. 40.
20 Ezra Pound to Viola Baxter Jordan, 14 September 1933, Beinecke Library, Yale University, New Haven, Connecticut.
21 H.D., *End to Torment*, p. 43.

Servants of Amor: The Early Poetry

1 Pound wrote to Dorothy Shakespear, on 13 July 1912, about "Psychology and Troubadours" that "the thing is bad but has paragraphs. It is utterly—as a whole—incomprehensible—but that was necessary. One can not write & convey information at the same time." Ezra Pound and Dorothy Shakespear, *Their Letters 1909–1914*, ed. Omar Pound and A. Walton Litz (New York: New Directions, 1984), p. 131. Difficult, if not incomprehensible, Pound's early correspondence with Dorothy might have provided a good deal more evidence for this study than it does if Dorothy hadn't practiced self-censorship, as the editors note: "We believe that between 25 and 30 of the earliest letters are missing, probably burned. Dorothy would have certainly destroyed the most personal ones. This would be quite in keeping with her practice in later life of cutting small sections from letters and destroying the rest" (p. 369). I noted lacunae at several points in the correspondence when it seemed that the subject of visionary eroticism might well have come up. For instance, on 12 September 1911 Dorothy writes, cryptically, "Yes. How are intimacy & mystery combined? Therein lies the whole root of the matter" (p. 57). What teases is that this is in response to a letter which, though it touches on the mystical, does not discuss the relation between "intimacy & mystery," but which does end with the editorial information *"rest of letter missing."* Still, the correspondence is valuable, not only for particular information, but for the general portrait it provides of the young Pound. Of greatest relevance for this study, the letters document the very large place of the occult in Pound's interests at that time. With respect to poetic composition, for instance, Pound wrote to Dorothy on 28 Oc-

tober 1911, "As for the rest I wonder if we can not look at the beginning of things as a sort of divine phantasmagoria or vision or what you will and the 'vagueness' etc as a sort of smoke—an incident in the much more difficult process of drawing down the light, of embodying it, of building it into the stiffer materia of actualities. The whole thing a process of art, of the more difficult art in which we are half media & half creators." *Their Letters*, p. 76.

2   G. R. S. Mead, editor of the theosophical journal *The Quest*, where Pound's "Psychology and Troubadours" first appeared.

3   Charles Williams, *The Descent of the Dove* (Grand Rapids, Mich.: William B. Eerdmans, 1972).

4   Ibid., p. 11.

5   Ibid., p. 12.

6   Ibid., p. 13.

7   Matthew Black, ed., *Peake's Commentary on the Bible* (London: Thomas Nelson and Sons, 1962), p. 958.

8   Ezra Pound, *Personae* (New York: New Directions, 1971), p. 148.

9   See Ian F. A. Bell, *Critic as Scientist: The Modernist Poetics of Ezra Pound* (London and New York: Methuen & Co., 1981), for a fascinating account of Pound's scientific metaphors. Bell demonstrates how current Pound's language was by unearthing not only many of Pound's direct sources, but by demonstrating as well the degree to which such language was "in the air." Bell argues that Pound's use of the language of science to describe extraordinary experience was a function of the author's relations with his audience—that Pound was simply searching for an acceptable idiom. According to Bell, "The problem, again, was that of the translation required by modernity: of finding an available lexicon for experience that was seemingly arcane and certainly private and communicatively unintelligible; of sustaining a public, and publishable, status for the myths of psychic or mystic phenomena" (p. 138). I find this argument convincing but incomplete. Pound, following the lead of the "trobar clus," hoped to be writing essays and poems that were available on two levels, one for the crowd, one for the elect. So there is always an element of obfuscation in his treatment of "mystic phenomena." Thus, Bell's insistence on Pound's desire to "seek a public voice" (p. 140) for such phenomena, his *"struggle* to maintain for the modern world the value of mystical perception" (p. 141), oversimplifies Pound's intent by collapsing Pound's two audiences into "the modern world." Walter Baumann is surely right in arguing for the "magical" in Pound's late as well as early work: "behind the formidable 'scientific' vocabulary the same magic continued." W. Baumann, "Ezra Pound and Magic: Old World Tricks in a New World Poem," *Paideuma* 10 (Fall 1981): 202–24. Much of Pound's science is veneer-thin.

10 Pound's willingness to see a "permanent basis in humanity" may have

been encouraged by Allen Upward. In *The Divine Mystery* Upward had said "I have to ask the reader to keep in mind that the earlier and later cults and beliefs that we have been considering flourished—as they still flourish—side by side, in the same geographical area, in the same city, and often in the same mind." A. Upward, *The Divine Mystery* (1915; rpt., Santa Barbara, Calif.: Ross-Erickson, 1976), p. 147. States of mind which once found a social expression persist without one, are recoverable.

11   Ezra Pound, "Terra Italica," in *Selected Prose*, ed. William Cookson (New York: New Directions, 1973), p. 56. For more on the *pecten cteis* see Peter Hamilton Laurie, "The Poet and the Mysteries," Ph.D. diss., Brown University, 1976, p. 5.

12   Pound is translating Leopardi's
     Desiderii infiniti
     E visioni altere
     Crea nel vago pensiere,
     Per natural virtù.

As printed in K. K. Ruthven, *A Guide to Ezra Pound's Personae* (1926) (Berkeley and Los Angeles: University of California Press, 1969), p. 80.

13   Consider, for example, this from the "Lingua Toscana" chapter of *The Spirit of Romance:* "here the preciseness of the description denotes, I think, a clarity of imaginative vision. . . . The Tuscan poetry is, however, of a time when the seeing of visions was considered respectable, and the poet takes delight in definite portrayal of his vision" (*SR*, 105).

14   In the "Introduction" to his translations of Cavalcanti Pound praised Cavalcanti's psychology, and reports a psychic state which is relevant to the last section of "The Flame"; namely, "that stranger state when the feeling by its intensity surpasses our powers of bearing and we [significant plural] seem to stand aside and watch it surging across some thing or being with whom we are no longer identified." Ezra Pound, *Translations* (New York: New Directions, 1963), p. 18.

15   Michael John King, ed., *Collected Early Poems of Ezra Pound* (New York: New Directions, 1976), p. 263.

16   There have been three recent Lacanian readings of Pound's sexuality: Alan Durant, *Ezra Pound, Identity in Crisis* (Brighton: Harvester Press, 1981); Paul Smith, *Pound Revised* (London: Croom Helm, 1983); Robert Casillo, "Anti-Semitism, Castration, and Usury in Ezra Pound," *Criticism* 25 (Summer 1983): 239–65. Although these three studies have their virtues, they do not address the occult dimension of Pound's sexuality. In a real way, then, their studies are strictly irrelevant in the context of my investigation. But, because they base their interpretations of Pound on many of the same passages that I deal with here, a few remarks about their work are in order. All three studies are highly critical of Pound and his work. Pound invites the ad hominem like no other poet in our tradition, and Durant, Smith, and Casillo exploit the opportunities. They

mean to explain Pound's more conspicuous failings, his fascism, anti-Semitism, and sexual chauvinism, in terms of the Lacanian version of the castration complex. While the translation into Lacanian terminology does provide a coherent frame in which to view Pound's "phallocentrism," it obscures Pound's own understanding of sexuality. When Pound's views diverge from the Lacanian model, they are left out (intentionally or not). So, the "erotic medium" escapes notice in oversimplifications like this: "The propriety of the sexual act, then, depends upon its function. If it is part of the process of natural productiveness then sexuality is celebrated; if not, then it is despised and condemned as perverted." Smith, *Pound Revised*, p. 55.

These studies are radically reductive. I am not sure whether the fault lies in the Lacanian perspective, or in the heavy-handed way in which Lacan is applied, but the result is the same. Readers who want to understand Pound are less likely to find passages like the following helpful than an impediment: "Rebuttal of genital privation by replacement of the penile appendage in women can enable the fetishist to renounce the fact of anatomical difference, and so partially forestall the field of the symbolic by superimposing this continued defensive captation of the ego upon a previous visual suppression." Durant, *Ezra Pound*, pp. 129–30. James Hillman (among others) has convincingly argued that psychoanalytic readings are themselves fictions, sometimes useful fictions, but not "facts." See J. Hillman, *Healing Fictions* (Barrytown, N.Y.: Station Hill, 1983), pp. 1–49. While Lacan, I suspect, generally observes the distinction, Durant, Smith, and Casillo do not.

It is symptomatic of these studies that Durant ends his investigation with "by no means an easy question": "If the *Cantos* cannot in any way be read as Pound intended, since the emergence of desire everywhere undermines the repression which sponsors conscious, didactic meanings, the question arises if there are any conditions at all in which the poem can be read with pleasure" (pp. 186–87). What is particularly telling is that Durant tries to answer this question *theoretically*, but that his reading of the poem leads him to such a question itself calls into question its usefulness.

I believe that critics interested in a psychological explanation of Pound's sexuality would do better to start with James Hillman, "Toward the Archetypal Model of the Masturbation Inhibition," *Loose Ends* (Zurich: Spring Publications, 1975), pp. 105–25.

17   Ruthven, *Guide to Personae*, p. 52. For a note on Pound's use of sources in "Coitus," see Peter Davidson, "Giulio Romano at the Spring Marriage," *Paideuma* 11 (Winter 1982): 503–10. Davidson appends photographs of Romano's sixteenth-century frescoes from the Sala di Psiche of the Palazzo del Te in Mantua, photographs which amply document Romano's style.

18 "Trace" occurs frequently, as in "Canzone: Of Angels," and "Canzon."

19 Pound, in the passage preceding this one, places "our" loss between Cavalcanti and Petrarch. Ezra Pound, "Cavalcanti," in *Literary Essays of Ezra Pound*, ed. T. S. Eliot (New York: New Directions, 1968), p. 154.

20 Pound describes this "passage" of the beloved in several early poems; it is, I think, the subject of the first stanza of "Canzon" and of "Gentildonna." It's interesting that Pound seems to favor kinetic over static representations of the beloved seen in the radiant world, though static images do occur, as in "Canzon: Of Incense," where the lady simply wears a "cloak of graciousness" that "gloweth" about her. This is consistent with Pound's characterization of the same reality as the "universe of fluid force," with the emphasis on fluidity.

21 The castle does appear in the second stanza.

22 For more inclusive readings of Pound's youthful poetic production, see Hugh Witemeyer's deservedly classic *The Poetry of Ezra Pound: Forms and Renewal, 1908–1920* (Berkeley and Los Angeles: University of California Press, 1969); Thomas H. Jackson, *The Early Poetry of Ezra Pound* (Cambridge: Harvard University Press, 1968), especially "The Poetic Moment" and "Thematic Geography" chapters, for placing Pound's poetry of moments in the tradition; and Stuart Y. McDougal, *Ezra Pound and the Troubadour Tradition* (Princeton: Princeton University Press, 1972), for the "troubadour" material. These books, and their many fellows, elucidate the context in which my more specialized investigations are to be understood.

23 G. R. S. Mead, *Simon Magus, An Essay* (London: Theosophical Publishing Society, 1892), p. 74.

24 Ibid., p. 75. P. L. Surette, in his "Helen of Tyre," *Paideuma* 2 (Winter 1973): 419–21, has also glossed Pound's footnote on Mead in *The Spirit of Romance* with Mead's booklet on Simon Magus; he assumes, however, that Pound accepted Mead's conclusion that to understand the sexual element in the Simon Magus legend as a literal history is error, while I have concluded that the burden of evidence suggests that Pound rejected it.

25 Williams, *Descent*, p. 13. Although I have chosen, in this chapter, to explicate Pound's remarks on the troubadours on their own terms, in the belief that they are most revealing when approached from this direction, it is not the only possible approach. Peter Makin, in his *Provence & Pound* (Berkeley: University of California Press, 1978), has collected a great deal of the background material, and although I think the danger of misreading Pound in light of his sources could be amply illustrated in Makin's book, there is a good deal of interest there for Pound scholars who desire to acclimatize themselves to Provence. However, Rene Nelli, in *L'Erotique des Troubadours* (Toulouse: Edouard Privat, 1963), who makes no reference to Pound whatsoever, is perhaps a more interesting

and indeed useful author, because Nelli's approach to the troubadours, which assumes an experiential basis behind the troubadour tradition, is more consistent with Pound's own. Nelli's researches can be very suggestive vis-à-vis Pound (see, for instance, pp. 166–67). However, to follow the suggestions through would take a separate study.

Divagation: Physiology

1 Ezra Pound, "Translator's Postscript," in Remy de Gourmont, *The Natural Philosophy of Love*, trans. Ezra Pound (New York: Rarity Press, 1931), and Ezra Pound, "The New Therapy," *New Age* 31 (16 March 1922): 259–60.

2 For a Lacanian reading of the "Postscript," see Durant, *Ezra Pound*, pp. 104–7.

3 Remy de Gourmont, *Letters to the Amazon* (London: Chatto & Windus, 1931), pp. 28–29. The French text runs: "On peut décrire l'amour chez les animaux, y compris l'homme considéré comme l'un d'eux, mais on ne peut pas décrire, autrement qu'en esquisses romanesques, l'amour humain. Il est possible de le montrer clairement en ses parties où il est commun à toute la nature; on ne peut dire clairement en quoi il est différent. On peut l'étudier systématiquement comme instinct, non comme sentiment." Remy de Gourmont, *Lettres à l'Amazone* (Paris: Mercure de France, 1922), p. 52.

4 See Richard Sieburth, *Instigations* (Cambridge and London: Harvard University Press), pp. 129–35, for a fuller explication of the book's tendentious character.

5 Gourmont, *Natural Philosophy*, p. 99. Pound has played up the humor of the original somewhat, in one of his rare departures from a literal rendering of the French text. See Remy de Gourmont, *Physique de l'Amour* (Paris: Mercure de France, 1906), p. 162.

6 Not all commentators think that Pound is being more than metaphorical in the postscript; Riddell, for instance, argues that "Pound's metaphors, which may appear more like a mystical physiology than a scientific text, cannot be taken literally, but can be read back into his theory of language and into his Imagist doctrine." Joseph N. Riddell, "Pound and the Decentered Image," *Georgia Review* 29 (Fall 1975): 573. While the latter is plausible, I must insist that the postscript is just what Riddell fears it is, "mystical physiology."

7 For the record, Pound insists he is not writing an antifeminist tract, and he says, "for the sake of symmetry [I] ascribe a cognate role to the ovule, though I can hardly be expected to introspect it"! (*NPL*, 170). Though this is, perhaps, just a clever way of insisting he *is* introspecting the male side of it. Perhaps H.D.'s *Notes on Thought and Vision* does "introspect" the woman's side of this. In any case, it is a fascinating text in its

own right, and it demonstrates that H.D.'s thinking about the place of
sexuality with respect to vision was not far removed from Pound's own
(without the strident masculinity of Pound's formulations). Of course,
the close parallels themselves suggest a shared understanding. H.D., *Notes
on Thought and Vision & The Wise Sappho* (San Francisco: City Lights
Books, 1982). For an excellent account of the limited place of the
woman in Pound's sexuality, see Smith, *Pound Revised*, pp. 43–46. The
antifeminist bias Smith delineates haunts every facet of Pound's thinking
about the erotic.

8 See later discussion in this chapter and Sieburth, *Instigations*, p. 146.

9 To keep the connotations of "metaphysics" clean, we should remember
that Pound wrote, "The term metaphysic might be used if it were not so
appallingly associated in people's minds with unsupportable conjecture
and devastated terms of abstraction" (*LE*, 151). Pound's metaphysics is
not abstract, but experientially grounded.

10 It is relevant to recall that the "radiant world" and the world of "fluid
force" appear to be synonymous in Pound's thought, so the transition
here is not really as unexpected as it might at first appear.

11 Christopher Smart, *The Collected Poems of Christopher Smart*, 2 vols.
(London: Routledge and Kegan Paul, 1949), 1:327.

12 Pound would remember these facts in the *Cantos*:

Windeler's vision: his letter file
        the size of 2 lumps of sugar,
but the sheet legible. Santa Teresa . . . [87/573]

13 The evolutionary element here—"not considering the process ended"—
applied to the future rather than the past, recalls Allen Upward's reflections in "The Plain Person," *The Egoist* 2 (February 1914): 47–49, with
which Pound would surely have been familiar:

I cannot myself understand how any thinking being who has accepted the
Darwinian revelation can believe that the natural process of evolution
stopped at the moment when the first anthropoid ape stood up on its
hind legs, and began to bark in articulate syllables. Not even a mission-
ary, nor a member of the Fabian Society, can seriously believe that all
men are alike externally. The most rabid philanthropist has not dared to
assert in so many words that all men look alike. But he foams at the
mouth if anyone insinuates in his hearing that they do not feel or think
alike. . . .

    The secret of all this absurdity, so far as I can make out, is that re-
cent evolution—the evolution of the last few thousand years—has gone on
mainly in the nervous system. [p. 47]

Although Pound might have paid particular attention to Upward's version of the idea, the idea itself was "current" and not limited to Pound's
circle. Upward, indeed, may have been influenced by Nietzsche.

14 Sieburth, *Instigations*, pp. 153–54; see also John Espey, *Ezra Pound's Mauberley* (Berkeley, Los Angeles, and London: University of California Press, 1974), p. 80; and Peter Hamilton Laurie, "The Poet and the Mysteries," p. 76.

15 Sieburth, *Instigations*, p. 153.

16 For the context in Propertius, see Prop. 2.1.4. In *The Cantos* Pound would play this note in a lighter key:

> Mr Elias said to me:
>   "How do you get inspiration?
> "Now my friend Hall Caine told me he came on a case
> "a very sad case of a girl in the East End of London
> "and it gave him an i n s p i r a t i o n . The only
> "way I get inspiration is occasionally from a girl, I
> "mean sometimes sitting in a restaurant and
>   looking at a pretty girl I
> "get an i-de-a, I-mean-a biz-nis i-de-a? [35/173–74]

17 For the likely literary sources, see Ruthven, *Guide to Personae*, p. 220.

18 Hugh Kenner, *The Pound Era* (Berkeley and Los Angeles: University of California Press, 1971), p. 63.

19 Gourmont, *Physique*, p. 97. Pound translated it, "What is good is what will continue to be." Gourmont, *Natural Philosophy*, p. 58.

20 For a succinct comment on the current status of the FitzGerald *Rubaiyat*, see Robert Graves's "The Fitz-Omar Cult" in *The Rubaiyat of Omar Khayaam*, trans. Robert Graves (London: Penguin, 1972), pp. 7–30. Of course, Graves thought Pound should be hanged.

21 This is Pound translating out of Gourmont's *Le Latin Mystique* (SR, 99).

22 Kenner, *Pound Era*, p. 256.

23 For an account of the general place of the glandular in Pound's thought, vis-à-vis Louis Berman's *The Glands Regulating Personality* (New York: Macmillan, 1921), see Bell, *Critic as Scientist*, pp. 211–14, and 221–22. However, Bell totally overlooks the degree to which Pound misreads Berman, *uses* Berman for his own ends.

24 "The New Therapy" appeared within a year of Pound's "Postscript."

25 Pound, "The New Therapy," p. 260.

26 Ibid., p. 259.

27 Ibid., p. 260.

28 Ibid., p. 259.

29 Ibid.

30 Ibid.

31 Ibid., p. 260.

32 Ibid.

33 Ezra Pound, notes for "Ur-Cantos," Beinecke Library.

34 Ezra Pound, "Three Cantos," *Poetry* 10 (June 1917): 120.

35 Kenner, *Pound Era*, pp. 417–18.

36 Pound, "Three Cantos," p. 118.

37 Pound recommended such "orderly visualization" to Dorothy Shakespear as a matter of practice in a letter of 21 November 1913: " 'Intellectual Vision' is, acc. Wm. Blake & others, the surest cure for ghosts. You'd better begin by seeing fire, or else by doing that visualization of points that I recommended." Pound and Shakespear, *Their Letters*, p. 277. Implicit in this letter is Pound's own status as a "present knower"; indeed, Dorothy's notebook entries from 1909 and 1910, collected in *Their Letters*, suggest that from the beginning she considered Pound a man of visionary experience.

38 Berman, *The Glands Regulating Personality*, p. 185.

39 Ibid., p. 181.

40 Ibid., p. 261.

41 Ibid., p. 91.

42 Ibid.

43 Manly P. Hall, *Man: The Grand Symbol of the Mysteries* (Los Angeles: Philosophers Press, 1937), p. 334.

44 Manly Palmer Hall, *Healing: The Divine Art* (Los Angeles: Philosophical Research Society, 1950), p. 219. The question of auras will be taken up later. The flickering of the aura is, of course, *spezzato*.

45 Ibid., p. 224.

"Cavalcanti": That the Body Is Not Evil

1 Kenner, *Pound Era*, p. 394.

2 The curious silence, in this context, of Pound on the Eleusinian mysteries, which he invokes as a caretaker of the way of the erotic medium in antiquity, cannot be explained as a change of heart on Pound's part. In the roughly contemporaneous "Terra Italica" (*SP*, 54–60) Eleusis occupies its usual place, and the "light from Eleusis" informs the understanding of the troubadours. The explanation for this apparent inconsistency is to be found, I think, in the aesthetic temper of the "Cavalcanti"; seemingly the knowledge that was embodied in Eleusinian ritual was not embodied in art. In any case, "the new thing" is not to be construed as a novel experience (inconsistent with a "permanent basis in humanity" anyway) but as a premier in art.

3 It should be clear that Pound is in no sense *for* licentiousness.

4 Pound, "The New Therapy," p. 260.

5 Upward, *The Divine Mystery*, p. 181.

6 Interestingly enough, "Patria Mia" of 1913 repeats the entire ideogram of the erotic medium: climate, gods, sexuality, and delay, the latter in the negative: "This new metropolitan has his desire sated before it is

aroused. Electricity has for him made the seeing of visions superfluous"
(*SP*, 104). Clearly Pound had already separated out the basic elements
of his thinking on the erotic medium at least twenty years before the
publication of "Cavalcanti."

7 Pound's sensitivity to the binding quality of the spurious idea may have
been quickened by his reading of *The Divine Mystery*, where Upward
maintains that "every positive system of philosophy, rationalist or religious, is an attempt to leave out the universe ['this invisible environment
in which we live']" (p. 3). Upward is everywhere alive to the experience
behind the representation, and it is a vividness Pound learned.

8 Pound, "The New Therapy," p. 260.

9 Upward, *The Divine Mystery*, p. 346.

10 With respect to the status of electricity, Pound's "possibly subtler form
of energy" probably echoes Upward's formulation: "The form of energy
called electricity is only the most coarse and obvious of the ethereal, and
doubtless also sub-ethereal, influences forever weaving the woof of Life
upon the warp of Matter." *The Divine Mystery*, p. 2. However, while
Pound may well have picked up the idea from Upward, it was "in the
air," at least in theosophical circles. For an American redaction, see
Manly P. Hall, *The Mystery of Electricity: A Retrospect and a Prophecy*
(Los Angeles: Manly Hall Publications, 1934).

11 Perhaps the lines "These poles [read genitals] are first in contact, and
after the current is generated we can gradually widen the distance between them" contain a veiled description of the logistics of this "mediumistic experiment," but the description is consistent with experiments
in the physics laboratory, at least as I knew them, so it is difficult to
gauge the specificity of the "illustration." For an account of Pound's use
of electromagnetism in this context *as analogy*, an analogy appropriate to
the day, see Bell, *Critic as Scientist*, pp. 40–42.

12 Pound said of Upward that "this author is a focus, that is to say he has
a sense of major relations. The enlightenments of our era have come to
him. He has seen how the things 'put together' " (*SP*, 405).

13 Allen Upward, *The New Word* (New York: Mitchell Kennerley, 1910),
p. 202.

14 Ibid., pp. 196–97. Donald Davie has used the vortex as a type of Pound's
poetic strategies in *The Cantos*, in *Ezra Pound* (New York: Penguin,
1976). My own attention to the substance of Upward's thought does not
exclude an interpretation along the line of Davie's. For recent, more inclusive accounts of the possible sources of Pound's vortices, see William
French and Timothy Materer, "Far Flung Vortices: Ezra's 'Hindoo'
Yogi," *Paideuma* 11 (Spring 1982): 39–53; and Bell, *Critic as Scientist*,
pp. 136–70. Clearly the vortex metaphor was current in many fields; however, I hold with Upward as the most proximate source.

15 Upward, *New Word*, p. 198.

16 Ibid., p. 208.
17 For a lucid account of Upward's influence on Pound, see Ronald Bush, *The Genesis of Ezra Pound's Cantos* (Princeton: Princeton University Press, 1976), pp. 97–100.
18 Upward, after all, lists fasting as a method of increasing sensitivity, presumably for Pound, "idiotic asceticism." We can say of Pound what he says of Cavalcanti, he "is eclectic, he swallows none of his authors whole" (*LE*, 159).
19 This is not a history of science, and I make no pretension to evaluate Pound's assertions against the science of today. The focus here is on Pound's characterizations of "modern" science and what he wants to set against it.
20 By, as he says elsewhere, the "magnetic" sense.
21 This too is the matter of a few minutes' experiment.
22 This is not to doubt the relevance of scientific theory, as in the case of Grosseteste, but the assumption must be that the theory is tested against the experience.
23 Luigi Valli, *Il Linguaggio Segreto di Dante e dei "Fideli d'Amore"* (1928; rpt., Rome: Libreria Antiguaria Bertoni, 1969).
24 In his 450-page book Valli only devotes 5 pages to Cavalcanti's canzone, and the analysis is rather perfunctory and reductive, beginning with the replacement of "Donna" with "un adepto," followed by more of the same. The paucity of analysis makes Pound's response seem, if anything, even more excessive.
25 I was unable to find either booklet in any American library, although I found a copy in Florence of *Sacerdotesse e Danzatrici nelle Religioni Antiche*, Biblioteca dei Curiosi, no. 51, ed. Edoardo Tinto (Rome: E. Tinto C., 1930).
26 Pound's phrase (*SP*, 55). The booklet in question is Nino Burrascano, *I Misteri di Mithra nell' Antica Roma*, Biblioteca dei Curiosi, no. 43, ed. Edoardo Tinto (Rome: E. Tinto C., 1929).
27 *Sacerdotesse*, p. 8.

The Cantos: First Assay

1 Ezra Pound to Homer Pound, 1 August 1928, cited in Angela Jung Palandri, "The 'Seven Lakes Canto' Revisited," *Paideuma* 3 (Spring 1974): 53.
2 Ezra Pound, holograph notes for Canto 25, Beinecke Library.
3 Pound seems unsure of the spelling, misspelling it at another point as "augeidos."
4 G. R. S. Mead, "The Augoeides or Radiant Body," *The Quest* 1 (July 1910): 705–25. The essay is reprinted, with minor revisions, as a chapter in the more readily available G. R. S. Mead, *The Doctrine of the Subtle*

Body in Western Tradition (Wheaton, Ill.: Theosophical Publishing House, 1967).

5   Mead, "Augoeides," p. 706.

6   Ibid.

7   Ibid., p. 709.

8   I here quote from the essay as collected in Mead, *Doctrine of the Subtle Body,* p. 35.

9   Pound, holograph notes for Canto 25, Beinecke Library.

10 Kenner, *Pound Era,* pp. 54–75.

11 Such as "her crotch like a young sapling" in 39/194, but that is, perhaps, simply simile.

12 Pound, holograph drafts for Canto 20, Beinecke Library.

13 In light of the preceding "physiological divagation" it is possible that "cortex" here refers not only to the tree but to the "evolutionary" effect of the experience on the lover's brain.

14 Ezra Pound, *Gaudier-Brzeska* (New York: New Directions, 1970), p. 145.

15 Tib.. 3.10.15. (Loeb translation).

16 Ezra Pound to Viola Baxter Jordan, 14 September 1933, Beinecke Library. He attributes the comparison to the "dark lady." Pound insisted on the dissociation in a letter of 17 April 1924 to William Bird as well, collected by D. D. Paige in *The Letters of Ezra Pound: 1907–1941* (New York: Harcourt, Brace and World, 1950), but the relevant sections were expurgated, presumably as offensive.

17 It is significant, surely, that Pound has "the flute" rather than "her flute."

18 As early as "Psychology and Troubadours" Pound had insisted on the possibility of a clean, but not visionary, sexuality: "In Catullus' superb epithalamium 'Collis O Heliconii,' we find the affair is strictly on one plane; the bride is what she is in Morocco today, and the function is 'normal,' and eugenic" (*SR,* 96). Of course, that he says "strictly on one plane" suggests that it could be on more than one.

19 As an index of the continuing density of our passage, it is worth noting that the phrase "gathered about her," used to describe the fauns, echoes the description of the hounds in Canto 17, cited earlier: "Leaping about her." Seemingly every phrase echoes another, or several others.

20 Durant, who also argues that the flute is phallic, seems to think "the fluid" here is "emission spilt on the grass." *Ezra Pound,* p. 182. Poets sing of many things, but not this.

21 Of course, even when Pound *intends* to be didactic he is often dauntingly difficult, as readers and critics alike attest. For an account of the nature of the difficulty Pound presents the reader, see James J. Wilhelm, *Il Miglior Fabbro: The Cult of the Difficult in Daniel, Dante, and Pound* (Orono, Maine: National Poetry Foundation, 1982). However, Wilhelm does not emphasize sufficiently, in his discussion of Pound, what he calls the "hermetic" element, the willful "opaqueness" of one who "does not

want to promulgate [his] ideas to the vulgar crowd" (p. 3). This is always an *additional* difficulty when Pound addresses the erotic medium.

22   Kenner, *Pound Era*, p. 422.

23   Ezra Pound, *Guide to Kulchur* (New York: New Directions, 1970),
p. 44. For an excellent account of the Neoplatonic resonance of *nous* for
Pound, see Sharon Mayer Libera, "Casting His Gods Back into the NOUS:
Two Neoplatonists and the *Cantos* of Ezra Pound," *Paideuma* 2 (Winter 1973): 355–77. Although Libera misconstrues the role of sexuality in
the experience of the *nous,* she is emphatic and correct in insisting on the
experiential ground of Pound's ideas. Her attempts to construct a metaphysics from Pound's "sources," Iamblichus and Gemistus Plethon, should
be weighed in light of Pound's adamant assertions that we no longer have
an "Aquinas map."

24   See Donald Davie, *Ezra Pound: Poet as Sculptor* (New York: Oxford
University Press, 1964), pp. 219–32, for the place of *forma* in Pound's
thought and poetics.

The Cantos: Second Assay

1   Kenner, *Pound Era*, pp. 454–58.

2   H.D. *End to Torment*, p. 23. See French and Materer, "Far Flung Vortices: Ezra's 'Hindoo' Yogi," p. 47, for (provisional) identifications of
the "series of Yogi books."

3   Ezra Pound, notes for Canto 20, Beinecke Library.

4   This is the Loeb text, which F. W. Cornish translates, albeit drably:
"Sirmio, bright eye of peninsulas and islands, all that in liquid lakes or
vast ocean either Neptune bears: how willingly and with what joy I re-
visit you, scarcely trusting myself that I have left Thynia and the Bithynian
plains, and that I see you in safety. . . ." Catull. 36.1–6.

5   Stock, *Life of Ezra Pound* (New York: Avon, 1970), p. 123. For Pound's
translation of the Flaminius tribute to Sirmio, see SR, 230.

6   Ezra Pound to H.D., May 1910, no. 169, D. D. Paige Collection, Beinecke
Library.

7   In 1911 Dorothy Shakespear asked Pound to build an "altar of stones"
for her at Sirmione, which he did (celebrated in "The Altar"), *Their
Letters*, p. 35. It was still there, "pink slablet uppermost," in 1913
(p. 199).

8   Pound to H.D., May 1910.

9   Ibid.

10   Ibid.

11   Ezra Pound to Homer Pound, dated Sirmio 1910, no. 170, D. D. Paige
Collection, Beinecke Library.

12   Paul Smith's Lacanian perspective makes him very sensitive to cloaked

(or imagined) appearances of the phallus in Pound's poetry. Thus, in Canto 47, " 'Io! Io!' might be taken as a graphic representation of male genitalia; the many 'Hast'ou' or 'Hast thou' refrains might be taken to transform phonologically to *hasta*, a spear; 'Two oxen are yoked for plowing' includes a sexual innuendo within its agrarian specificity; 'The stars fall from the olive branch' clearly alludes to male ejaculation." Smith, *Pound Revised*, p. 53.

13 Kenner, *Pound Era*, p. 143.

14 There are, as well, a number of references to the topography of the Lake Garda region merely by name, particularly in the later cantos: Gardone, Gardasee, Brescia, and so on.

15 Curiously enough, there is an echo of Pound's experiences at Garda in "The Serious Artist," in his distinction between the two "cults" in the arts, the cult of beauty and the cult of ugliness: "As there are in medicine the art of diagnosis and the art of cure, so in the arts, so in the particular arts of poetry and literature, there is the art of diagnosis and there is the art of cure. They call one the cult of ugliness and the other the cult of beauty. The cult of beauty is the hygiene, it is sun, air and the sea and the rain and the lake bathing. The cult of ugliness, Villon, Baudelaire, Corbière, Beardsley are diagnosis. Flaubert is diagnosis" (*LE*, 45). Lake bathing, in Garda, is the suspicion. What is particularly interesting here is the emphasis on "cure," which in *The Cantos* will become the "gt/healing." The passage suggests the oscillation in Pound's own work between "the delineation of ugliness" and "Beauty" which "reminds one what is worth while" (*LE*, 45).

16 Pound, for his own reasons, appropriates the ruins of the temple of Jupiter at Terracina on behalf of Venus. See Leon Surette, " 'A Light from Eleusis': Some Thoughts on Pound's *Nekuia*," *Paideuma* 3 (Fall 1974): 204. Surette's reflections on the role of Eleusis in Pound's *Cantos* as subject and as a "paradigm" of their action are brought together in his *A Light from Eleusis: A Study of Ezra Pound's Cantos* (Oxford: Oxford University Press, 1979).

17 Pound linked the Latin phrase to his desire to rebuild the statue when he juxtaposed the two epigraphs to the "Religio" section of his *Selected Prose*.

18 Kenner, *Pound Era*, pp. 333–38.

19 Ibid., pp. 335–36.

20 For a lucid reading of Pound's views on the Albigensians see Peter Makin's chapter "The Heretics of 'Provence' " in *Provence & Pound*, pp. 217–55. Makin overturns many misreadings of Pound perpetrated by scholars who have carelessly interpolated current scholarly opinion into their understanding of Pound. Makin starts with Pound's views and holds fast. In his exposition of Pound's Albigensians, Makin sketches quite accurately the basic outlines of Pound's thinking about sexuality in Provence.

However, Makin's focus on Pound's "position" vis-à-vis his sources obscures the ramifications of Pound's preoccupation with the potentialities of sexuality. As a result, Makin's observations are limited to an understanding of Pound's Provence. He does not seem to suspect the much larger place of extraordinary sexuality in Pound's work as a whole.

21 He could joke about "Manichaeans," at least in letters. In a verse epistle to Marianne Moore, in which he teased her about his—to her—libidinous exploits, he called himself a Manichaean. Pound to Moore, 1 February 1919, no. 517, D. D. Paige Collection, Beinecke Library.

22 See Surette, " 'A Light from Eleusis,' " and Laurie, "The Poet and the Mysteries." Laurie's study is excellent if lyrical.

23 Leon Surette sums it up: "It should be understood that the Mysteries remain a mystery to this day." " 'A Light from Eleusis,' " p. 201.

24 Ibid., p. 197.

25 Laurie concludes, as well, that sacred coition—in Pound's mind—was part of the mysteries. "The Poet and the Mysteries," p. 4.

26 That the mysteries at Eleusis were celebrated in the autumn does not seem, for Pound, to have presented any contradiction in his sacred calendar. For an account of Pound's synthetic chronology, see Surette, " 'A Light from Eleusis,' " p. 205.

27 Ezra Pound, notes to Rock-Drill, Beinecke Library.

28 Stock, *Life of Ezra Pound*, p. 122.

29 Ibid. Actually, Pound wrote "altar," and went on to insist that it was time to bring the gods back—a significant, and in light of this analysis, predictable ellipsis. Pound to Bride M. G. Adams Scratton, undated, Beinecke Library.

30 Pound's letter to Bride Scratton, as cited in Stock, *Life of Pound*, p. 122.

31 Pound, notes to Rock-Drill, Beinecke Library.

32 The passage from Canto 27 from which this line comes is problematical; a good many of our radicals are present, but they are combined with "tovarisch" and the Russian Revolution in ways I don't understand.

33 Pound's identification for Zagreus is in the notes to Canto 25, Beinecke Library.

34 See Laurie, "The Poet and the Mysteries," pp. 188–93.

35 The "spiriti" again recalls the discussion in Pound's "Cavalcanti."

36 Pound there asserted that "Anatole France, in his commentary on Horace's 'Tu ne quaesaris,' has told us a good deal about the various Oriental cults thronging the Eternal City" (SR, 96). I have not been able to locate the France commentary, but the context of Pound's remark suggests that it bears on our subject. In these passages from Canto 91 the meaning of the quotation seems self-evident.

37 Wendy Stallard Flory, "The 'Tre Donne' of the Pisan Cantos," *Paideuma* 5 (Spring 1976): 45–52. Readers interested in the personal dimension of Pound's work will find Wendy Stallard Flory, *Ezra Pound and The Can-*

tos: A Record of Struggle (New Haven and London: Yale University Press, 1980), an invaluable resource.

38 The publication of H.D.'s *End to Torment*, however, at least calls for a reexamination of the evidence. H.D., perhaps, has a place here. William French, in " 'Saint Hilda,' Mr. Pound, and Rilke's Parisian Panther at Pisa," *Paideuma* 11 (Spring 1982): 79–87, also argues for H.D.'s place among the *Tre Donne*.

39 D. S. Carne-Ross, "The Music of a Lost Dynasty," *Boston University Journal* 21 (Winter 1973): 25–41.

40 Ibid., p. 33.

41 I here cite the translation of the "Cavalcanti" essay (*LE*, 155–56) rather than that of Canto 36—interested readers may compare.

42 John Hamilton Edwards and William W. Vasse, *Annotated Index to the Cantos of Ezra Pound* (Berkeley and Los Angeles: University of California Press, 1957), p. 12.

The Cantos: Third Assay

1 Alan Durant realizes that the paradise of Pound's poem is embodied in Pound's own idiom of sexuality: "the interrelation of amor, the eye, and the flame or crystal." *Ezra Pound*, p. 171. Durant understands this as "an apotheosis of the phallus," arguing that "these various instances enact a resistance to castration whose polyphonic and pervasive presence is woven in this final network of association centering on the flame, the eye, the crystal, and in gemmology, the close of the poem in paradise" (p. 173).

2 The exact resonance of "spirits" here is difficult to determine. To fathom it one would have to take into account the likely derivation from Pound's "Cavalcanti" and the "spirito" of "Donna Mi Prega" which Pound glosses out of Avicenna: "Ibn Sina, for *spiriti*, *spiriti* of the eyes, of the senses" (*LE*, 158). Pound's references to Avicenna, however, are difficult to trace, so difficult that I had almost given up hope of tracking down "Amplius in coitu phantasia," which Pound attributes to the *"seicento* edition of the *De Almahad* of Avicenna" (*LE*, 176), when Colin McDowell wrote to suggest Avicennae, *Philosophi Praeclarissimi ac Medicorum Principia*, first published in Venice in 1546, reprinted by Greg International, Westmead, Farnborough, Hants., in 1969. Though the title and dates are off, "Amplius in coitu phantasia" does appear on pp. 81 and 88, and it can safely be assumed that this is Pound's source. The *spiriti* remain a puzzle.

3 In all this there is a loud echo of the realm of fluid force.

4 Ezra Pound, notes for Canto 25, Beinecke Library.

5 Pound and Shakespear, *Their Letters*, p. 288.

6 H.D., *End to Torment*, p. 17.

7 French, in "Saint Hilda," pp. 79–87, argues that Pound's cats are derived from Rilke's "Der Panther," but although this attribution is attractive and plausible on the surface, Pound's cats are, I think, first his own. In any case, Rilke's panther is image as picture, while Pound's cats figure extraordinary experience (just as "The Tree" is not about the tree in the yard, Pound's panther is not about any panther in a zoo). Rilke's influence is no more than incidental.

8 Reed Way Dasenbrock traces *spezzato* to Dante's *Commedia* in "Dante's Hell and Pound's Paradisio: 'tutto spezzato,' " *Paideuma* 9 (Winter 1980): 501–4.

9 Presumably the passage Pound has in mind from the *Convivio* is 3.8.2:

> *I say, then, that, having explained the sentence of that part in which this lady is praised as regards her soul, we must proceed, and see how, when I say "That which we read in her sweet countenance," I praise her as regards her body. And I say that in her countenance appear things which "speak to us of the joys of Paradise." The most noble [of all joys], and that which is written as the end of all the others, is to be content, and this to be blest; and this pleasure truly lies in her aspect, because, in looking upon her, people find content, so sweetly does her beauty feed the eyes of the beholders. But not as in Paradise, because the contentment which is perpetual cannot to any [here] be such.*

This translation is from Dante Alighieri, *The Banquet* (*Il Convito*), trans. Katharine Hillard (London: Kegan Paul, Trench Co., 1889), pp. 173–74.

10 Kenner, *Pound Era*, p. 45. The passage from Upward runs as follows:

> *How hard the old cloistered scholarship, to which the Nobels of a bygone age gave their endowments, has toiled to understand the word glaukopis, given to the goddess Athene. Did it mean blue-eyed, or gray-eyed, or—by the aid of Sanskrit—merely glare-eyed? And all the time they had not only the word glaux staring them in the face, as the Athenian name for owl, and the name of the ox-eyed Hera to guide them, but they had the owl itself cut at the foot of every statue of Athene, and stamped on every coin of Athens, to tell them that she was the owl-eyed goddess, the lightning that blinks like an owl. For what is characteristic of the owl's eyes is not that they glare, but that they suddenly leave off glaring, like lighthouses whose light is shut off. We may see the shutter of the lightning in that mask glaukos. And the leafage of the olive, whose writhen trunk bears, as it were, the lightning's brand, does not glare, but glitters, the pale under face of the leaves alternating with the dark upper face, and so the olive is Athene's tree, and is called glaukos. Why need we carry owls to Oxford?[Upward, New Word, p. 238]*

11 Upward, *New Word*, p. 238, my emphasis.

Concluding Informally

1   H.D., *End to Torment*, p. 21.
2   Ibid., p. 18.
3   Ibid., pp. 54–55.

Index

Abelard, Peter, 21
"Abelard" (Pound), 21, 22
Agassiz, Louis, 65
Albas, 81, 105
Albigensians, 14, 40, 101, 103, 147
  n.20
"Apparuit" (Pound), 22
Apollonius of Tyana, 106, 112
Arnaut. *See* Daniel, Arnaut
"Arnold Dolmetsch" (Pound), 76
Atasal, 115–16, 121
Augoeides, 72–75, 79, 84, 91, 119
Avicenna, 149 n.2

Bacon, Roger, 64
Baudelaire, Charles, 37
Baumann, Walter, 135 n.9
Bell, Ian F. A., 135 n.9, 141 n.23,
  143 n.11
Berman, Louis, 25, 39–42, 46–47,
  49, 141 n.23
Blake, William, 142 n.37
"Blandula, Tenulla, Vagula"
  (Pound), 97, 98
Botticelli, Sandro, 62, 109
Browning, Robert, 45
Bush, Ronald, 144 n.17
Byron, Lord, 7

The Cantos (Pound), xi, 71–128
  passim, 130, 137 n.16, 140 n.12,
  147 n.15; acorn in, 28, 35; and
  "Cavalcanti," 67, 114–15; crystal
  in, 119–22; dawn in, 104–6; Eleusis
  and Montségur in, 101–4; and exact perception, 65; exoteric and
  esoteric, 85; extraordinary experi-

ence in, 44–45; eyes in, 109–13;
flame in, 119–20; gods, status of
in, 123–25; in H.D.'s *End to Torment*, 4, 6; incense in, 106–8;
light in, 48, 119–22; luminosity in,
125–26; Sirmione in, 96–98; subjective experience in, 117–28 passim; Terracina in, 98–100; *individual cantos:* Canto 2, 108, 112, 119,
122, 125; Canto 3, 44, 97, 98,
124; Canto 4, 117, 121, 124; Canto
5, 98, 128; Canto 7, 56; Canto 12,
82; Canto 14, 82; Canto 17, xii,
81, 106, 145 n.2; Canto 20, 77,
95, 107–8; Canto 21, 80, 120,
128; Canto 23, 121; Canto 25,
70–91 passim, 93, 94; Canto 27,
108, 109, 148 n.32; Canto 29, 81,
117; Canto 35, 141 n.16; Canto
36, 101; Canto 39, 5, 89, 99, 105,
120, 145 n.11; Canto 45, 82;
Canto 47, 97, 147 n.12; Canto
63, 107; Canto 74, 88, 95, 101,
106, 114, 115, 117, 125, 127;
Canto 76, 95, 100, 114, 115, 121,
122, 124; Canto 77, 97; Canto
78, 117; Canto 79, 5–6, 105,
125, 126; Canto 80, 109, 129;
Canto 81, 113; Canto 83, 1, 102;
Canto 87, 28, 140 n.12; Canto
90, 107, 122; Canto 91, 105, 111,
112, 120, 121, 122; Canto 95, 93,
122; Canto 97, 105, 106; Canto
98, 119; Canto 100, 110, 120,
122; Canto 106, 110; Canto 107,
97, 121; Notes for Canto 111,
110, 119; Canto 113, 81, 119;
Canto 116, 122; Canto 120, 118

Biographical Note

Kevin Oderman is currently an assistant professor of English at the University of Nebraska in Lincoln. He has published criticism on a wide range of modern and postmodern authors, and his literary essays and poems have appeared in such journals as *Paper Air* and *Origin*.

Library of Congress Cataloging-in-Publication Data
Oderman, Kevin, 1951–
  Ezra Pound and the erotic medium.
  Bibliography: p.
  Includes index.
    1. Pound, Ezra, 1885–1972—Criticism and interpreta-
tion.   2. Sex in literature.   3. Erotic poetry,
American—History and criticism.   I. Title.
PS3531.082Z784   1986   811'.52   86–11471
ISBN 0–8223–0672–7